POETRY
OF
DOROTHY L. SAYERS

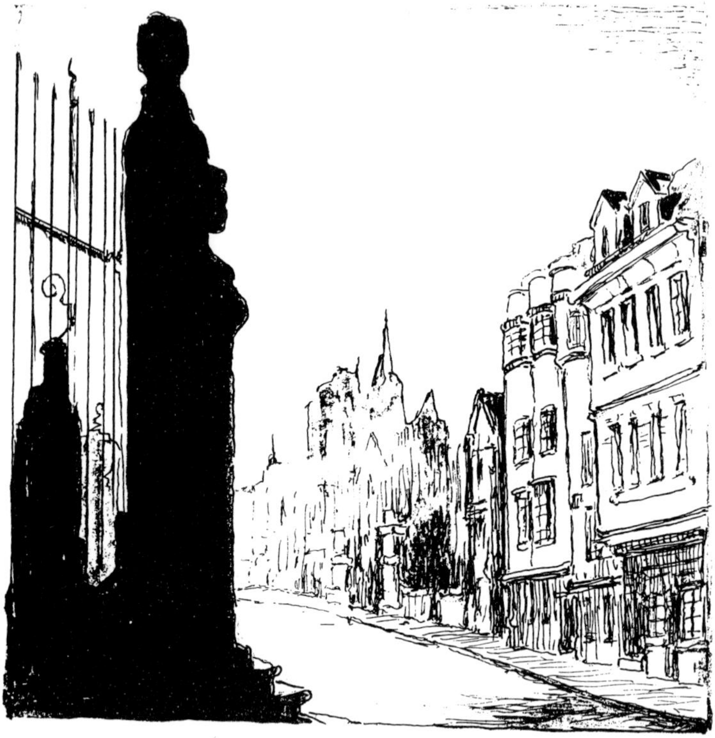

POETRY
OF
DOROTHY L. SAYERS

♣

CHOSEN AND EDITED BY
RALPH E. HONE

WITH A PREFACE BY
BARBARA REYNOLDS

DRAWINGS BY
NORAH LAMBOURNE

"Now from the grave wake poetry again,
O sacred Muses I have served so long!"
Purgatory, i, vii – viii

THE DOROTHY L. SAYERS SOCIETY
IN ASSOCIATION WITH
THE MARION E. WADE CENTER

First published in Great Britain in 1996
by The Dorothy L. Sayers Society
in association with
The Marion E. Wade Center.

© 1910, 1915, 1916, 1918, 1919, 1921, 1934, 1935, 1937, 1939, 1940, 1942, 1943, 1944, 1953, 1962, 1973, 1981, 1996 The Trustees of Anthony Fleming deceased
© This compilation copyright 1996 Ralph E. Hone

All rights reserved. No part of this publication may be reproduced, stored in a retrieval system or transmitted at any time or by any means, electronic, mechanical, photocopying, recording or otherwise, without prior permission of the copyright holders.

ISBN 0 9518000 2 7

British Library Cataloguing-in-Publication Data
A catalogue record for this book is available from the
British Library

Designed by Geoff Green and produced
at Silent Books Ltd, Swavesey, Cambridge CB4 5QG
Typeset in Garamond
Printed in Great Britain
by Redwood Books,
Trowbridge, Wiltshire

CONTENTS

♣

Acknowledgements	ix
Preface by Barbara Reynolds	xi
Introduction	1
List of Poems in This Edition	21
Texts of the Poems, with Annotations	23
Listing of All Poetry by Dorothy L. Sayers and Where Located	160
Index	167

ABBREVIATIONS

Brabazon	James Brabazon, *Dorothy L. Sayers: A Biography* New York: Charles Scribner's Sons, 1981
Hannay	Margaret P. Hannay, ed *As Her Whimsey Took Her* Kent, Ohio: Kent State University Press, 1979
Reynolds	Barbara Reynolds, *Dorothy L. Sayers: Her Life and Soul* London: Hodder & Stoughton, 1993

ACKNOWLEDGEMENTS
♣

My first acknowledgement is to thank Mr. Bruce Hunter of David Higham Associates, London, the agents for the Dorothy L. Sayers copyrights, for offering me the opportunity to collect and edit her poetry.

My next expression of gratitude must go to Dr. Barbara Reynolds. Our friendship developed from a mutual interest in the life and work of Sayers and has covered a quarter of a century. I wish to thank her especially for much valued assistance. Her biography, which appeared to great acclaim in the centenary year, is bound to become in many of its aspects a definitive portrait. My thanks are also directed to her as Editor of *SEVEN* for granting me permission to use material from my essay in the Sayers Centenary issue. Time after time, she has answered queries helpfully, sent me materials she had discovered, and encouraged my own efforts in research. Most of all, I thank her for kindly writing a Preface to this work. She is, of course, not liable for any lapses on my part.

Members of the Dorothy L. Sayers Society in England have always shown their encouragement. I should like to thank especially Col. Ralph Clarke, President Emeritus; Mr. Christopher Dean, Hon. Chairman; and Miss Norah Lambourne for her delightful drawings.

The kind assistance of many expert librarians must be mentioned: Mr. Fred Hearth, Director, and Mrs. Sandra Richey of the Armacost Library of the University of Redlands; Dr. B. C. Barker-Benfield, Mrs. Melissa Dalziel, Dr. Judith Priestman, and Mr. Mark Purcell of the Bodleian Library, Oxford; Mr. Duncan G. Heyes of the British Library, London; Miss Maria Croghan of St. Hilda's Library, Oxford; Dr. Larry Burgess, Director, A. K. Smiley Public Library,

Redlands, California; Miss Ruth Mortimer, Curator of the Rare Book Room of the William Allan Neilson Library of Smith College, Northampton, Massachusetts; Miss Pauline Adams of Somerville College Library, Oxford; Mrs. Marjorie Lamp Mead, Associate Director of the Marion E. Wade Center of Wheaton College, Wheaton, Illinois.

I am also very grateful for acts of kind assistance by friends and colleagues: Professor Beatrice Batson, Professor F. S. Bromberger; P. D. James; Dr. Hannah Leckman; Mrs. Beth Melonuk; Miss Roxanne Starbuck; Professor Alvis Lee Tinnin; Professor Dora Van Vranken; Mrs. Laura Vroman; Mr. Laurence Wormser.

My wife Harriet Hall Crawford Hone has been constantly at my side, assisting in tasks which my relative immobility threatened otherwise to frustrate. To her I acknowledge my deepest obligations; in relation to any Wimsey context, she is *my* Harriet.

Additional acknowledgements will be found in the Notes to the Introduction and in Annotations to the poems.

PREFACE
BY BARBARA REYNOLDS

♣

To many readers this book will come as a surprise. Dorothy L. Sayers, detective novelist, dramatist, lay theologian: in these capacities she is widely known, but as a poet she remains to be discovered. Yet she wrote poetry all her life, from her talented beginnings as a child to her last years as the translator of Dante. Her first two books, published by Basil Blackwell, were volumes of poetry; many of her poems were printed in journals; others were circulated privately, sometimes as presents to her friends. Selected, edited and annotated for the first time, they take their place at last among her other writings, on which they shed new light.

 She began as a poet and to read her poems now is to realize, with a shock of new awareness, that she always remained one, even in her prose works. Her imagination responded creatively to the heroic and the romantic. In the apparently ordinary she disclosed the strange and the unexpected. The prosaic details of murder, police investigations, clues and finger prints are invested in her stories with the magic of unreality. The more realistic the setting, the more powerful the transference to an imaginary world. Lord Peter Wimsey, the fair-haired sleuth who solves all problems, assisted by his faithful attendant – what is he but a poetic fiction, one of the knights errant, accompanied by his squire, who captured her imagination as a child and later as a student of medieval romance? This is one explanation of his enduring fascination. Both real and unreal, he shares with Sherlock Holmes the immortality of legend.

 Pattern always attracted her. In her poems, as in her detective stories, she trained herself to master form. That was the key which unlocked the power of words. From an early age she understood this instinctively. She loved the incantation of rhyme; she experimented with metre; she played with unusual words; she practised the fixed forms, sonnet, ballade, triolet, finding them a liberation rather than a restraint – one sign of a poet. Her study of early French literature led her on to still more elaborate structures, especially that of the "lay", a labyrinth of interlinking poems, resulting, when achieved, in the beauty of complexity resolved. The example included here shows her mastery of an intricate skill. Poetic themes recur in her later writings, and phrases from the poems are re-echoed. She also employed an intriguing complexity in the remarkable "Obsequies for Music", a work she evidently hoped might be set to music. It is surprising that it never was. Now that it has been made available perhaps it will be. Readers of her other works will be intrigued to discover that the ringing of bells had long charmed her with its formal pattern; that the crafts of architecture and of writing were early linked in her mind; that the treatment of the artist's agony of making, as in "The Poem" and the noted sonnet in *Gaudy Night*, anticipates some aspects of *The Mind of the Maker*.

In her later years Dorothy L. Sayers asserted that her only approach to religious belief was via her intellect. Her poetry shows that this had not always been the case and perhaps was never entirely so. A sense of joy and wonder is the starting point of several of her religious poems, notably in *Catholic Tales and Christian Songs* (1918).

Read against her personal background, her poems illumine various stages in her life. It is significant that there are few poems extant for the period 1921-1926, the time of her deepest unhappiness, when, like Harriet Vane's, her "singing voice" was stifled. It was perhaps re-awakened by the work she resumed on her translation of the Anglo-Norman poem *Tristan*, in 1929. While working for S. H. Benson's, she employed her verbal skill in composing advertising jingles. Word play and literary games were among the hobbies she shared with like-minded friends, for one of whom she composed a series of brilliant pastiches of sixteenth-century poetry.

A re-commitment to serious poetry was induced in 1937 by an invitation to write a verse drama for Canterbury Cathedral. *The Zeal of Thy House* and its successor, *The Devil to Pay*, represent an important advance in her maturity as a poet. A firm sense of direction gives a lapidary resonance and strength to her lines. This, to use her own phrase, is no longer the "poetry of search", but the "poetry of statement". There is strength, too, in her war poems, the most characteristic being "The English War", published in *The Times Literary Supplement* in 1940 and anthologised several times in company with poems by C. Day Lewis, Stephen Spender, Laurie Lee and other well-known contemporaries. At this period she tried her hand at free verse, in a conversational style which underplayed and, indirectly, reinforced the realities of war, as in "Aerial Reconnaissance", and "Target Area" (one of her most moving poems). Among her playful verse of this period are the delightful cat poems, including the mock Virgilian "Aeneas at the Court of Dido", perfect in form, diction and style.

The influence of Dante on her own poetry is found especially in *The Just Vengeance*, the verse drama she wrote for Lichfield Cathedral (1946) and which she considered her best work. It is also reflected in a poem written privately for friends, perhaps one of her most beautiful and original: "For Timothy, in the Coinherence." It fittingly concludes and crowns this collection.

Dorothy L. Sayers, poet: she founded no school, nor did she slavishly follow one. Her poetry, individual and personal, has the marks of her period, her education, her reading, her literary tastes, her constructive skills and her imaginative power. Above all, it communicates her love of words, of pattern, and of the English language. There is much in it to be discovered and enjoyed. We owe thanks to Professor Ralph E. Hone for his heroic task and for his loyal editing.

BARBARA REYNOLDS
Cambridge, England 1996

INTRODUCTION

I

Dorothy Leigh Sayers (1893-1957) is probably best-known to the reading public as a detective-story novelist and the creator of the noble sleuth Lord Peter Wimsey. From 1923, when Wimsey was first introduced to readers in *Whose Body?*, through 1937, when he was presented as a married man in *Busman's Honeymoon*, and until World War II, Sayers went from strength to strength as a purveyor of increasingly subtle and ingenious plots involving her hero in ten novels and parts of three volumes of short stories. Along the way she produced other detective-story works – one non-Wimsey novel, one successful Wimsey play, several collaborative efforts with fellow-members of The Detection Club, innumerable lectures and articles, and four collections of detective stories, revealing herself as an authoritative figure in the history of detective fiction.

But Sayers, like many other able writers, had tried her hand successfully in several other genres, among them apologetics, drama, journalism, juveniles, literary criticism, translation, and poetry. Indeed, the first two books she published were volumes of poetry: *OP. I* (1916) and *Catholic Tales and Christian Songs* (1918). Slightly more than two years before her death, she wrote to her Oxford friend Professor C. S. Lewis (8 August 1955) to complain out of her perceptive self-knowledge:

> Only a few people take my verse-making seriously. I am pigeon-holed as a mystery-monger who in old age has taken to tinkering in an amateur way with religion and rhyme. I'm not really supposed to know anything about it. Which shows that one should always go on as one began – otherwise nobody will believe that one began that way.[1]

Bluntisham Rectory where Dorothy lived as a child.

One should demur from her half-jesting final opinion in these remarks, but no one can deny the accuracy of her claim to long-standing familiarity with "religion and rhyme."

Early on she had had serious intentions of earning her laurels by writing poetry. This prospect was not entirely accidental. Her clergyman father detected her early-childhood fascination with words and music. She acknowledged in *My Edwardian Childhood*, her unfinished autobiographical sketch (*ca.* 1932), the "sheer gorgeousness of Jabberwocky," Lewis Carroll's nonsense verse in *Through the Looking Glass*, which her father read to her in their home in Brewer Street, Oxford. "Many things," she wrote, "that I could only dimly understand were delightful to me by reason of rhyme or rhythm."[2] Besides the Alice books, her father introduced his daughter to Latin and to music. Her mother, whose intuitive awareness of education was far in advance of her time, taught her to read and discovered that rhymes and pictures were the viable tools of her teaching. As Mrs. Lammas recognized in *Cat o' Mary*, the unpublished and incomplete "straight" novel (with pronounced autobiographical touches) which Sayers started around 1934, anything that rhymed could be poured wholesale into her daughter's memory and would stick there like glue. In due time, governesses guided Dorothy farther into the life of poetry in French and in German. And visits and correspondence with her cousin Ivy Shrimpton greatly encouraged her poetic achievement.

Much of this has been established by Sayers's son John Anthony Fleming in his Preface to James Brabazon's biography of his mother: "When Dorothy herself died in 1957, I found that she had kept ... numerous exercise books full of childhood poetry, drawings, plays and stories, often embellished with coloured drawings and fancy lettering, the earliest complete volume dating from early in 1908, when she was not yet fifteen years old...."[3] Barbara Reynolds, in her biography of Sayers, is more detailed:

> As well as acting, producing plays and making costumes and props and programmes, in addition to regular hours with her governess, Dorothy was also writing long narrative poems, some of which she illustrated in pen-and-ink or watercolour.... When she has time, she makes copies to send [to Ivy]. In a letter dated 23 February 1908 she says she is at work on a complex poem, "Songs of the Crown," divided into sections, one being entitled "Lyrics of War" and another "The Prisoner of War."[4]

Reynolds also notes the existence of other projects of Sayers in this period of her youth: ballads about a Sir Roland, several cantatas (inspired by *The Three Musketeers*), cantos of *The Comediad*, a verse comedy *The Wit*, another named *Aldovrando*, and poems in French.[5]

There is no uncertainty about Sayers's poetic accomplishments when, at fifteen, she commenced her schooling at Godolphin in Salisbury. The school magazine contains several examples – her first published verse. Other examples are to be found in letters of the period sent to her parents. Some products she kept close by her to be shared in Oxford days with a Somerville friend, Catherine Godfrey ("Tony"), and a young poet friend, Giles Dixey.

She also tackles the subject of poetry in *Cat o' Mary*. Katherine Lammas summarizes her chances of success in attending Beaufort School (modeled on Godolphin):

> she was a poet, & that was surely rather unusual. She didn't write sentimental little verses, either, about moonlight & roses, but good stalwart stuff; cavalier songs, & ballads.... And she knew it was good verse, with metre that required no apology. Metre was one of the things she knew about, instinctively, just as she knew about English syntax....[6]

Salisbury Cathedral where Dorothy was confirmed

In school she was guided into reading and study of most of the English classics, especially in lyric and narrative verse; while already at home she had read Milton, Pope, Samuel Butler, Beddoes, Scott, Jane Austen, Dickens, and Wilkie Collins; and she was familiar with many of Shakespeare's plays. She had also found intense excitement in Dumas and Molière, both at home and again at school. She would have been instructed in the Arthurian cycle, the ballads and legends of Britain, the historic events that engendered in literature patriotism and rectitude. There was always accessible the collateral rich fiction which influenced the development of character. An insatiable reader like Dorothy L. Sayers could easily find literature dominating life.

Sayers *did* excel academically at Godolphin. She won the Gilchrist Scholarship in Modern Languages enabling her to enter Somerville College, Oxford, in Michaelmas Term 1912. In a sense, the caged bird was then set free. The young lady who had revealed herself as good in self-analysis met an educational tradition which prided itself on precise analysis of all matters. The somewhat aloof observer of other people and their putative motives became by training discriminating in taste and opinion, and learned to become dispassionate in offering conclusions, always obliged to substantiate her judgments. The word-hungry admirer of English, French, and German romanticism produced lyric after lyric. Much was merely experimental, especially pursued to master set forms of sixteenth-century French poetry. Much dealt with the common ventures of life – companionship, service, affection, sudden change, sudden death – to all of which she gave sensitive utterance. Some dealt with classical mythological or folkloristic subjects replete with allegorical depths. Much was sheer effusion, written for fun. Much of it pertained to Oxford, as to the hub of the universe. She was especially adept at narrative verse.

Chivalric romance strongly controlled her world of imagination. It was at the core of her living recreationally in the stories of Alexandre Dumas. It abounded in her reading and formal study. It was prominent in the images of her poetry. It provided an atmosphere for love and sexuality. Her religious life and attitudes were also affected: King Jesus represents much the same kind of fantasy and panoply of ideals. She was, withal, intrigued by the labyrinthine ways of good and evil.

The period of Sayers's most prolific production and publication of verse came in the years 1915-1921, just after she had completed her university education. These years may be thought of as part of her Oxford years, even though during one of these years she lived and taught in Hull and for another year she lived and served in Normandy as a bi-lingual educational associate of Eric Whelpton. She drew her inspiration from Oxford. It was the place of her greatest achievements. It was associated with her closest friendships. Its stones and spires marked her most beloved geography. After almost every tour of duty elsewhere, she returned to Oxford.

This was the period in which she issued her two volumes of verse (*OP. I* [1918], *Catholic Tales and Christian Songs* [1919]). This was the period in which she saw her poetry appear in *The Fritillary, The London Mercury, The New Witness, The Oxford Chronicle, Oxford Journal Illustrated, Oxford Magazine,* and *The Saturday Westminster*

Gazette. This was also the period in which she contributed to and edited Blackwell's publications: *Oxford Poetry, 1915* (containing poems by Aldous Huxley, Dorothy H. Rowe, and J. R. R. Tolkien, among others, as well as Sayers); *Oxford Poetry, 1917* (including poems by Muriel St. Clare Byrne, E. R. Dodds, Una Ellis-Fermor, Robert Graves, Aldous Huxley again, Helen Simpson, and Doreen Wallace, among others, as well as Sayers); *Oxford Poetry, 1918* (with poems by Basil Blackwell, Miss Byrne again, Aldous Huxley still once more, Eleanora Geach, and again Miss Wallace, among others, as well as Sayers); and *Oxford Poetry, 1919* (with poems by Vera Brittain, J. B. S. Haldane, Vivian de Sola Pinto, and Miss Wallace again, among others, as well as Sayers). This was also the period in which she contributed to a long narrative poem to each of two volumes published by Blackwell under the title *The New Decameron* ("The Journeyman" [1919], "The Master-Thief" [1920]).

Professor de Sola Pinto has personally characterized the Oxford poetry-publishing scene for the years 1919-1921:

> At this time almost every Oxford undergraduate had literary ambitions. Some of my own verses were printed in student periodicals and I received much encouragement from the inclusion of several of them in the annual undergraduate anthology called *Oxford Poetry*, where I appeared in the company of a select band that included L. A. G. Strong, Dorothy Sayers and C. H. B. Kitchen. Perhaps I was rather foolishly elated by the sight of my verses in the chaste print of these volumes, but at least it gave me the pleasant sensation of having a place, however humble, in the great Oxford Parnassus.[7]

Near the beginning of this period, on 8 October 1915 – just three months after she had completed her university work, Dorothy L. Sayers wrote from Bluntisham a letter to Dorothy H. Rowe, her very close Somerville friend, accompanying a "bulky package" of poems. The letter makes several references to Oxford, and the tone of nostalgia is pronounced. It was fitting that the letter with the package of poems should carry slight shop-talk, the craft-judgments of one poet to another. Sayers wrote:

> The rondeaux especially are the merest technical exercises in most cases – trying different shapes & models with different lengths of line & arrangement of rime & refrain – none original, as you will see.

They are the sort of thing one either tears up when done, or keeps filed for reference in an alphabetical list. The last poem "Matter of Brittany" was written merely for enjoyment. I thought I was tired of "Oxford" & "Alma Maters" & "Going-downs" & "To a Leader of Men's" & things that meant a powerful lot, & terseness & pregnancy & dignity & so on, so I thought I'd just revel a bit in the dear old obvious glories of scarlet cloaks & dragons & Otherworld Journeys & in the clank & gurgle of alliteration, & the gorgeousness of proper names.[8]

II

When Dorothy Sayers returned from her year in Normandy at L'Ecole des Roches, she had already decided (as Eric Whelpton has recalled), to follow the beckoning new attraction of detective-fiction-writing. Her decision was reached through the practical pressure to earn her own way as a writer. She certainly felt the pinch of necessity and was determined not to go on being a charge to her parents.

Like her own Hilary Thorpe in *The Nine Tailors*, she was pragmatic enough to know that she had to concentrate on the best way to acquire a dependable income. When Sir Henry Thorpe put forth the query "What are you going to write? Poetry?" she responded:

> "Well, perhaps. But I don't suppose that pays very well. I'll write novels. Best-sellers. The sort that everybody goes potty over...."[9]

Professor Lewis Thorpe – not at all fictional! – offered an amusing comment, which sheds light on Sayers's predicament, when he called attention to the announced publishing policy attached to the Blackwell *Adventurers All* series (found on the back page of Sayers's *OP. I*, Number Nine in the series). The publisher had boasted of his subsidy of the series "to remove from the work of young poets the reproach of insolvency". Professor Thorpe took deliberate aim at the statement offered by Blackwell: "It is hoped that these Adventurers may justly claim the attention of those intellects which, in resisting the enervating influence of the novel, look for something of permanent value in the more arduous pursuit of poetry." Professor Thorpe wrote: "It seems unlikely that Dorothy Sayers's share of the 2/- for which each copy [of *OP. I*] was sold can have removed her work from 'the reproach of insolvency'; but this her failure to resist 'the enervating influence of the novel' was soon to do."[10]

It should be noted that Hilary Thorpe did not abruptly nor finally abandon her muse. Late in *The Nine Tailors* (1934) she writes to Lord Peter:

> I am writing a poem about the founding of Tailor Paul [one of the ring of bells in Fenchurch St. Paul]. Miss Bowler says it is quite good and I expect they will put it in the School Magazine.[11]

So with Sayers. Lord Peter stalked into her life and writing, and like Sayers herself, he enjoyed verse. A Balliol man with an enviable academic, social, aristocratic, military, bibliophilic, musical, and financial reputation, he could indulge at the least provocation in doggerel or parody or limerick; and he became adept at jingles (as do "Death Bredon" and Montague Egg in Sayers's fiction). He could, moreover, weave into his remarks borrowed poetic phrases and cadences.

In his early appearances Lord Peter is only a poetaster. For all his presumed awareness, say, of alliteration and assonance ("cadaveric lividity, rigidity, and all the other quiddities"), he reveals little sustained sensitivity to serious poetry and remains committed "to the sacred duty of flippancy."

What is significant about the development of his character in this respect, however, is that his creator could not allow her love of verse to vanish. As she followed him in the detective novels, she even staged forays into verse as narrator: witness, for example, the bell-mottoes and the tomb inscription in *The Nine Tailors*. When she came to *Gaudy Night* she subjected the craft of verse-writing to rare analysis, and, among other things, produced a sonorous sonnet – the tandem work of Harriet Vane and a refurbished Lord Peter. He no longer posed as a comedian.

In the last novel, he even kneels before his wife, quotes lines from John Donne's "The Anniversary," and manifests a new aspect of his character by saying: "How can I find words? Poets have taken them all, and left me with nothing to say or do."

One could say that Lord Peter to begin with was something of "a lunatick," he then became a lover, and at last he became a poet.[12]

III

Barbara Reynolds has shown that the invitation to Sayers to try her hand at religious drama came unexpectedly – even before the launching in London of the successful detective-play *Busman's Honeymoon* in December 1936.[13] Her reputation as a detective novelist was firm enough, but she was "recognized" by the public as a dramatist only after the success of the Wimsey play, and that acclamation she shared with her collaborator Muriel St. Clare Byrne, who was certainly better known in professional theatre circles than Sayers. "The Mocking of Christ," included in *Catholic Tales and Christian Songs* (1918), had not been widely circulated; and to those who did know of the twenty-year-old dramatic poem, its style and content might have seemed unpromising to associate with the Canterbury Festival program starred by T. S. Eliot's *Murder in the Cathedral* (1935).

Charles Williams's *Thomas Cranmer of Canterbury* was the play produced at the Festival in 1936. It was the recommendation of Williams that triggered the solicitous approach to Sayers by Miss Margaret Babington, the Festival organizer and the steward and treasurer of the Friends of Canterbury Cathedral, in a letter dated 6 October 1936.[14]

At first Sayers exhibited reluctance to accept the invitation to produce a play for the Canterbury Festival because of the weight of other obligations. However, when she had read Miss Babington's book, *The Romance of Canterbury Cathedral*, and the medieval Latin chronicle by Gervase of Canterbury about the rebuilding of the Choir after the devastating fire in the twelfth century, she yielded.

After an interval of twenty years, the almost incredible had materialized. Years before in Oxford she had written poems evocative of medieval settings and religious values. Deterred at the time from continuing exclusively in writing poetry by the expectation of inadequate financial returns, now financially secure and widely known as a successful detective-fiction-novelist, she was being *invited* to produce a play open to medieval focus and to verse, if she chose. Both her immediate predecessors in the Festival had employed verse. She did choose, and *The Zeal of Thy House*, with memorable passages, was presented at the Canterbury Festival in 1937.

Her love of drama and theatre, now whetted by the success of the play *Busman's Honeymoon*, encouraged Sayers to devote herself to the construction of an absorbing plot; to the development of vivid and forceful characters propelled by distinct conflicts; to the underscoring of an ancient and timeless theme; and to the articulation of a commanding dialogue. The poetry is magisterial in its imagery and music. The fact that the entire work was imbued with Sayers's religious and spiritual sensitivity guaranteed its distinction.

More religious dramas by Sayers were to ensue. Canterbury requested a second, *The Devil to Pay* (1939). She wrote for B.B.C. a play to be aired on Christmas Day 1938, *He That Should Come*. Consequently, the B.B.C. commissioned a series of plays on the life of Christ, *The Man Born to be King* (1943). After the end of World War II, Lichfield Cathedral commissioned a play as part of its 750th anniversary, *The Just Vengeance* (1946). And for the Festival of Britain in 1951, she wrote *The Emperor Constantine*, produced in Colchester and in London.

In all these productions she set forth convictions on subjects perennially vital to people of spiritual discernment. She bravely challenged the feckless stereotyping of the Main Character in the New Testament story. And the writer who made a generation aware that the dogma *is* the drama would not allow the siphoning away of the Atonement and the Divinity. Her verse in each case bears the vigor of the didactic. But with the exception of some peripheral passages I have omitted in this collection poetic portions from her dramas.

Sayers's experience in drama was so keen that she knew a well-written play on a most pertinent theme with excellent settings and dialogue needs still a flourish of magic to make it truly enthralling: it requires an inspired director and *dramatis personae*. Thus, in the prefatory pages of *The Devil to Pay* she included a sonnet "To the Interpreter Harcourt Williams."

Harcourt Williams had been the producer of *The Devil to Pay* and played Faustus. He had also "created" William of Sens in *The Zeal of Thy House* and performed the part of Caspar, King of Chaldea, in the London National Transmission from Broadcasting House of

Sayers's *He That Should Come*. He was also to participate in the first, seventh, and eighth plays of *The Man Born to be King* in 1943.

The sonnet is an excellent example of a vibrato structure: it swings from potential to actual, from organ to function, from commodity to use; but the controlling idea is that a play (though possibly "sound," "light," "Souls' conference," "Gold," "speech") is only complete when a talented actor animates it. There are lines in this sonnet of amazingly crisp summary; the closing couplet with its strong spondaic pattern is superb:

> *Thus, then, do thou, taking what thou dost give,*
> *Live in these lines, by whom alone they live.*

The poetry in *The Man Born to be King* is slender by comparison with the plays which preceded it and with those that follow it. There is a fourteen-stanza poem of simple quatrains entitled "The Makers," printed among the prefatory material of the published play-cycle. It is a variation on the theme of "To the Interpreter," very fluid but not as striking in style. (A portion of this poem was appropriated by the Girl Guides with the author's permission.)

IV

England's involvement in World War II spurred Sayers to use verse patriotically and, occasionally, sardonically. She commanded, cajoled, and criticized in order to urge her fellow-citizens to be alert and supportive of war-time leadership. "The English War" portrayed the heroic stance of the island nation which had had a long, illustrious history of resisting tyranny and of defending freedom. The poem was widely circulated among British forces; it earned respect because of its strong, positive phrasing. The author used plain talk: she spoke of "*men who love us not, yet look / To us for liberty*"; of the allies who abandoned England; of those who were but "*waverers.*" She offered some startlingly fresh imagery:

> No dangerous dreams of wishful men
> > Whose homes are safe, who never feel
> The flying death that swoops and stuns,
> The kisses of the curtseying guns
> > Slavering their streets with steel.

Its five-line stanzas were memorized and recited as slogans in the old Gaelic sense.

Sayers could sometimes achieve emotional catharsis in war-time by unpacking her heart in words of harsh judgment and disdain; this was the character of a couple of poems which she even forgot about in a few years. Less strident but no less straightforward is her contribution to an anthology compiled by her friend Storm Jameson, *London Calling*. In this patent appeal by a large number of British writers for global support of England in the fight against totalitarianism and aggression, Sayers's poem "Lord, I Thank Thee" is an amusing, light-hearted recapitulation of what she has learned from Necessity. It is composed in free verse and comes across as a conversational, whimsical expression of war-time by reference to non-belligerent items – the economic restraints of rationing, coupons, scarcity of commodities, and the patriotic conservation of petrol and coal.

"Aerial Reconnaissance" is a dramatic monologue in free verse, remarkable for its portraiture of an apparently dispassionate or stoical Fenland observer of photographs of war-bombing demolition. The height from which the photographs were taken creates the illusion of utter aloofness. The observer sees only *things* – houses, power-stations, ships, harbors, dikes, lands awash, machines – *no persons*, because they are too small and insignificant to be seen in the photographs. There is confessed admiration for both the aerial reconnaissance and the destruction: that is giving technology its due. If he is stoical, the observer may be reining in overt emotional reaction because Memory may recall the appallingly painful releasing of Fenland waters. The poem reminds us of Sayers's skill in presenting character in her fiction by close and undeviating attention to subject.

Sayers decided to speak behind the persona of a cat in her wartime poem "War Cat." This decision proved to be so satisfying in her eyes that she resumed the stance on later occasions. "War Cat" begins with pity for a cat obliged to submit to wartime food restrictions, proceeds to an imagined feline response, and passes on to a denunciation of cat-stealth, only finally to be tempered by another display of pity. The poem is, of course, a beast-fable written for humans who need their perspectives improved. Sayers uses free verse and conversational tone.

In 1944 Sayers published "Target Area," a dramatic monologue in free verse studded with irony. It is a reflection evoked by a brief but poignant news item: "*Our bombers / were out over Germany last night, in very great strength; / their main target was Frankfurt.*" The target area was associated in the poet's mind exclusively with the home of her Godolphin School Music Mistress Fräulein Fehmer; years previously she had returned to her home in Germany. Beyond the note of appreciation for her teacher, and over the evidence of Sayers's gifts to her Music Mistress, and aside from the expression of a solicitous concern for Fräulein Fehmer's living conditions in Germany, there is the report of Fehmer's confession that she had, back in Germany, become "an ardent Nazi": this completely altered the relationship.

Sayers then faces all the discernible consequences: Was Fehmer's well-known admiration of Chopin "politically correct" in Nazi Germany? Did she have any feeling for the "agony of Poland," the target of Nazi aggression? Did she endorse the blitzkrieg and the bombing of London, among other English cities? Was she distressed by the military reversal of the Nazis in the U.S.S.R.? How did she react to the reciprocal endurance of "the death sent out" returning? Sayers's conclusion is truly supranational: "all men stand convicted of blood / in the High Court"; "the solidarity of mankind is a solidarity in guilt." There is an ironic counterpoint of musical imagery in this recital of personal acquaintance.

In the last year of the War, Sayers produced another cat poem but privately as a Christmas greeting for her friends. In solemn quatrains, "Aeneas at the Court of Dido" progresses through twenty-two stanzas of mock-epic quality following an "Argument" ("A cat having suffered many misfortunes in an enemy-occupied sea-coast town, at length escapes to a British naval raider, and, after a prosperous voyage, is brought to a sea-port in England"). The "hard-bitten Tom" relates to the new English "Dido" his tale of "famine, fear, and pestilence" in a far-off "Troy," his experience of enduring bombing and devastation, and his rescue by "foreign gods" (who wore British naval uniforms). This Aeneas-cat finally sums up the world's plight:

> ...Cat's eyes may not avail
>   To pierce the awful pantry-door
> Where Justice in her iron scale
>   Weighs out the meed of less and more.
>
> Enough that some dark deed of shame
>   By cats has set all Heaven at odds;
> For these prodigious woes proclaim
>   That there is war among the gods.

At the beginning of the global conflict, Sayers produced a series of "Wimsey Papers," and in the last item (published in the *Spectator* in January 1940) she has Peter write to Harriet in the unmistakable terms of Sayers speaking to herself:

> You are a writer – there is something you must tell the people, but it is difficult to express. You must find the words.
> Tell them, this is a battle of a new kind, and it is they who have to fight it, and they must do it themselves and alone. They must not continually ask for leadership – they must lead themselves.

Sayers tried.

v

Sayers's final poetic endeavors lay in verse translation. Not, certainly, that this was a new development. She wrote in 1957 that "The passion for verse-translation [was] a kind of congenital disease" with which she had been afflicted all her life – "that is, I began to suffer from it as soon as I was able to think in any language but my own." At school, when asked to make simple translations of French or German set passages, she harried herself to produce proper metrical translations. At her Somerville College scholarship examination, she tackled a Petrarchan sonnet in the French Unseen presented to her and claimed to be forever thereafter haunted because she had rendered under pressure of time one line in a "revolting cliché," "ruining the effect of the following line, which was quite a good one." She recollected spending valuable time on a chorus from the *Hecuba* by Euripides, rendering it "into fluent and undistinguished iambics" – all merely as an exercise in preparation for a Responsions examination! Her final examination, The Schools, provided her with another sonnet which tripped her up because she offered "a miserable sprig of rue ... in place of heliotrope" in her zeal to render metrical translation. Her training at Oxford lay largely in translating medieval French poetry; and when she completed her undergraduate work, she "embarked" on a translation of *The Song of Roland*, "in rhyme instead of assonance" (which she remedied in the Penguin Classics edition published in the last year of her life); she also produced a translation of *Tristan in Brittany* (in couplets), published first in excerpts in *Modern Languages* in 1920 and then, *in toto*, in 1929 by Ernest Benn.[15]

Dante was, of course, to be the major luminary for her. The story of how this developed – by the partial influence of Charles Williams again, the serendipity of her starting to read Dante during an air-raid, the devout effusion from an epiphany this produced in her, the pre-emptive attention she gave to him, and her unflagging attention to the translation – has been adequately told.[16] Her translation of the *Inferno* was published in 1949 and of the *Purgatorio* in 1955. Her death in December 1957 forestalled her completion of the *Paradiso*, but her friend Barbara Reynolds finished it for her, complete with Introduction and Notes, in 1962. She had delivered several Dante lectures; many of them were gathered up into two volumes of Dante studies and published before her death.

On 8 May 1956, when she spoke to the Cambridge University Italian Society, she lamented that "in confused times like our own ...one can count upon no common background of belief or feeling."[17] She spelled this out in detail in another lecture, "The Translation of Verse," delivered to the Oxford University English Club on 6 March 1957. "When translating any ancient author," she said,

> it is now no longer possible, as it was at one time, to rely upon the reader's ability to recognize at sight an allusion to classical myth, Bible history, Arthurian legend, the astronomy of the visible heavens, and other standard sources of the poet's inspiration. The passing away of compulsory Latin and Greek, or regular churchgoing and religious instruction, the shift of interest from folk-lore and natural history to sociology and the abstract and mechanical sciences have

made the understanding of literature much more difficult, even for those who have received a liberal education. Moreover, the translator has to consider a whole class of new readers who have received nothing but a technical training, and need to have the path into the literary past made smooth for them.[18]

She welcomed, therefore, the opportunity to be allied with Penguin Classics. All that she had pin-pointed as evidence of cultural limitation she had herself been privileged by birth, training, and temperament to enjoy. Her task was to share with others less fortunate. This awareness accounts mainly for the comprehensive introductions, the copious and illuminating notes, the clear diagrams (contributions of C. W. Scott-Giles)[19], the helpful glossaries, and the infectious vigor of Sayers's Dante translations.

The year after her death, *The Times Literary Supplement* published an editorial honoring her motive and accomplishment as a translator of Dante.

> Her main energies in her last years were devoted to translating and expounding Dante, having in mind that wide new audience for serious writing which is "literate" rather than "educated." For that task, into which she put much zest, good will, and ingenuity, she deserves our permanent gratitude....
>
> Recognizing that Dante is "the most profound, the most subtle, the most civilized, the most Catholic, the most intellectual and the most exalted of all Christian poets," Miss Sayers also recognized that to the new reading public she describes he is "a poet whose living voice is made inaudible to them by an alien language, an alien cosmology, and six intervening centuries of religious and political confusion." Miss Sayers made a valiant attempt to bridge this gap in her introduction and notes to her Penguin versions of the *Inferno* and the *Purgatorio* and in her actual translation she recognized that she was writing for a public who would never make an attempt to read Dante in the original.... She wanted her version to be alive, and alive in a contemporary way, in its own right.[20]

To avoid the vexing problem of what to offer from the immense Dante-translation effort of Sayers in this collection, I have included only "St. Bernard's Hymn to the Blessed Virgin." This passage from the *Paradiso* was first printed privately as a 1949 Christmas greeting for Sayers's friends. Barbara Reynolds very graciously and wisely incorporated this passage in the Penguin translation of the *Paradiso* which she completed in 1962.

As to Sayers's other major translations of verse – *Tristan in Brittany* and *The Song of Roland*, I have omitted representation. There are, however, several minor occasional poems in translation which reveal her deftness and taste.

VI

A collection of papers by Dorothy L. Sayers was prepared by her son John Anthony Fleming with the aid of Muriel St. Clare Byrne, her literary executrix, and published posthumously in 1963 by Gollancz in London. The collection was published under the title of the first essay, *The Poetry of Search and the Poetry of Statement*. That paper had been given as a lecture to the Cambridge University Italian Society on 8 May 1956. It reveals some significant aspects of her thoughts on the nature of poetry held in the last years of her life.[21]

Sayers, as some others have observed, may have been too categorical in making this identification of types of poetry. It is obvious that her preference is for Poetry of Statement; the connotation of the language she uses betrays her judgment. Yet she specifically stated that *both* types can be good poetry. Undoubtedly she was slanting her remarks toward her pre-emptive esteem for Dante and *The Divine Comedy*: he is surely *the* Poet of Statement *par excellence*.

Her opinion of literary critics seems not to have wavered from what she sternly held a decade earlier, when she wrote to C. S. Lewis (24 October 1948):

> May I seize this occasion to trot out a hobby-horse and a grievance? There is to-day far too little interpretative criticism. Everybody insists on doing "creative" criticism – which means that the critic simply uses his author as a spring-board from which to leap off into an exposition of his own views about the universe…. There is no doubt a place for this kind of thing. But I still think we need the pure interpreter, who will sit down before a poem, or whatever it is, with humility to it and charity to the reader, and begin by finding out and explaining what the author actually *did say* before he starts to explain what the author ought to have said and would have said if he had

been as enlightened a person as his critic. A friend of mine, after toiling through several unintelligible books about modern poetry, said plaintively: "I want a critic who will say, 'This is a poem about a bus; this is what the poet says about the bus; this is the conclusion the writer draws from his observation about the bus; I think he has said it well (beautifully, badly, etc.) for the following reasons.' After that he can say what he likes, and I shall know where I am."[22]

VII

Great diversity characterizes Sayers's verse. All of her youthful compositions were form-conscious. Indeed, she was fascinated by medieval and Renaissance set-forms in poetry, not only in school and university days but all through her life. She was also challenged by stanzaic varieties. Also, she would have admitted unapologetically that some of her verse was ephemeral: she loved to write purely for fun. (The repertoire of the singing voice should be varied.)

In her religious plays she often turned to blank or to free verse, where the imagery and metric patterns supplied effective appeal. Much of her incidental poetry relating to World War II anxieties appeared in conversational style reminiscent of her detective-fiction dialogue successes. Cats may be as useful as heroes for uncomplicated meditative subjects. But, while expecting tolerance for her "light" poetry, she certainly hoped that her more serious efforts in drama or in translation would be accepted appreciatively by discriminating readers.

Sayers knew especially well how to put music into her poetry. This may be recognized not only in her adroit use of the common echo-devices and mellifluence of language but also in her variety of cadences. It must be remembered that composers, some outstanding, were employed to provide musical settings for her work and responded ably: Benjamin Britten, Robert Chignell, Antony Hopkins, G. H. Knight, and most recently Simon Hancock.

She always trained a critical eye on substance as well. She was inveterately curious about most matters that touched her life; time and time again she may be seen pursuing a topic until she makes it her own. Her poetry, accordingly, makes for exactitude.

VIII

My purpose in presenting this collection of poetry by Dorothy L. Sayers is to offer for the first time the opportunity to many readers to examine her verse efforts for themselves. The arrangement is chronological so that the development of themes and techniques may the more easily be assessed. Heretofore many of Sayers's poems have been fugitive. Some have been kept in private collections. Some were published in elusive publications. Her own first volumes of poetry were published in slender editions. The religious plays and the later verse-translations (which manifest special talent) were issued in larger numbers and may be found in libraries. The Annotations are designed for those whom Sayers described as "curious" about such things; they are not to be taken as patronizing.

RALPH E. HONE
*Redlands, California **1996***

NOTES

1 Letter of Dorothy L. Sayers to C. S. Lewis dated 8 August 1955. The original is in the Marion E. Wade Collection, Wheaton College, Wheaton, Illinois, and is cited by permission.
2 Quoted in Barbara Reynolds, p. 7.
3 Anthony Fleming, "Preface," James Brabazon, p. [xi].
4 Reynolds, p. 22.
5 *Ibid.*, p. 24.
6 Dorothy L. Sayers, *Cat o' Mary*, p. [94]. The manuscript original is in the Marion E. Wade Collection, Wheaton College, Wheaton, Illinois; cited by permission.
7 Vivian de Sola Pinto, *The City That Shone* (London: Hutchinson, 1969), p. 266. I am indebted to Barbara Reynolds for calling my attention to this item.
8 Quoted in Ralph E. Hone, *Dorothy L. Sayers: A Literary Biography* (Kent, Ohio: Kent State University Press, 1979), pp. 21-22. The original letter of Sayers to Dorothy H. Rowe is now possessed by the Bodleian Library, Oxford.
9 Dorothy L. Sayers, *The Nine Tailors*, The First Part: Mr. Gotobed Is Called Wrong with a Double.
10 Hannay, ed., p. 111.
11 *The Nine Tailors*, The Seventh Part: Plain Hunting.
12 See my article "From Poetaster to Poet: One Aspect of the Development of Lord Peter Wimsey," *Seven* X (1993), 43-58.
13 Reynolds, pp. 273-274.
14 Charles Williams garnered an impressive reputation as a novelist, a dramatist, a

poet, a literary critic, a writer of biography, and a man of pronounced theological and ethical assurance. He had read Sayers's *Catholic Tales and Christian Songs* with approval as early as the time it was published, and he had greeted *The Nine Tailors* rhapsodically. Usually a man of terse, compact statement, he could at times be exuberant. If this was his style in recommending Sayers to Miss Babington as a potential Canterbury Festival play-writer, he must have had superb intuition regarding her ability to produce successfully in another genre beyond detective fiction.

15 "The Translation of Verse,: *The Poetry of Search and the Poetry of Statement* (London: Gollancz, 1963), pp. [127]-128.
16 C. S. Lewis, ed. *Essays Presented to Charles Williams* (Oxford: Oxford University Press, 1947), pp. [1]-2; especially Barbara Reynolds, "Introduction," *Paradise* (Harmondsworth, Middlesex: Penguin, 1962); Reynolds, *The Passionate Intellect: Dorothy L. Sayers' Encounter with Dante* (Kent, Ohio: Kent State University Press, 1989); and, of course, Reynolds's centenary biography.
17 "Dante the Maker," *The Poetry of Search and the Poetry of Statement*, p. [21].
18 "The Translation of Verse," in *ibid.*, p. 135.
19 However, the frontispiece of *Purgatory* is by Norah Lambourne.
20 Professor Gilbert F. Cunningham also commended Sayers for her Penguin translation, and, while he noted that "few reviewers have given it unqualified approval," he very fairly honored the evidence of her thorough work. Gilbert F. Cunningham, *The Divine Comedy in English*, 2 vols. (Edinburgh and London: Oliver and Boyd, 1965, 1966), II, pp. 211, 219-220.
21 Dorothy L. Sayers, *The Poetry of Search and the Poetry of Statement and Other Posthumous Essays on Literature, Religion and Language* (London: Gollancz, 1963). There are twelve essays in the collection: ten of them were produced in the last five years of Sayers's life; seven had also been previously published, two of them in *Nottingham Mediaeval Studies* (II, 1958), edited by Professor Lewis Thorpe. All of them, which contain her clearest statements on poetry and translation of verse, were lectures she had been invited to give to various groups all over the country.
22 The original letter is in the Marion E. Wade Collection of Wheaton College, Wheaton, Illinois, and is cited by permission.

THE POEMS

✣

1. THE GARGOYLE (1908 ?), p.24
2. TO SIR ERNEST SHACKLETON (1910), p.25
3. CAPTIVO IGNOTO (1910), p.25
4. PEREDUR (1912), p.27
5. THE HORN (1912), p.32
6. TO H.P.A. (1914), p.36
7. TO A LEADER OF MEN (1915), p.47
8. TO MEMBERS OF THE BACH CHOIR ON ACTIVE SERVICE (1915), p.48
9. ICARUS (1916), p.51
10. THOMAS ANGULO'S 'ÐEATH' (1916), p.51
11. LAY: MUMMERS, LET LOVE GO BY, *OP. I* (1916), p.54
12. THE LAST CASTLE, *OP. I* (1916), p.62
13. THE THREE KINGS, *OP. I* (1916), p.71
14. MATTER OF BRITTANY, *OP. I* (1916), p.72
15. A MAN GREATLY GIFTED, *OP. I* (1916), p.74
16. THE ELDER KNIGHT, *OP. I* (1916), p.75
17. HYMN IN CONTEMPLATION OF SUDDEN ÐEATH, *OP. I* (1916), p.80
18. EPITAPH FOR A YOUNG MUSICIAN, *OP. I* (1916), p.81
19. TO M. J., *OP. I* (1916), p.82
20. LAST MORNING IN OXFORD, *OP. I* (1916), p.83
21. ΠΑΝΤΑΣ ΕΛΚΥΣΩ, *Catholic Tales* (1918), p.84
22. ÐEAD PAN, *Catholic Tales* (1918), p.86
23. REX ÐOLORIS, *Catholic Tales* (1918), p.88
24. SACRAMENT AGAINST ECCLESIASTS, *Catholic Tales* (1918), p.90
25. BYZANTINE, *Catholic Tales* (1918), p.91
26. PYGMALION (1918), p.92

27. THREE EPIGRAMS (1919), p.94
28. FOR PHAON (1919), p.96
29. SYMPATHY (1919), p.97
30. VIALS FULL OF ODOURS (1919), p.97
31. OBSEQUIES FOR MUSIC (1921), p.98
32. THE POEM (1921), p.105
33. ON GUINNESS (1935), p.106
34. HERE LIES THE BODY OF SAMUEL SNELL (1934), p.107
35. SONNET, *Gaudy Night* (1935), p.108
36. AUPRÈS DE MA BELLE (1937), p.109
37. THE ZODIACK (1937), p.111
38. TO THE INTERPRETER (1939), p.119
39. THE ENGLISH WAR (1940), p.120
40. LORD, I THANK THEE – (1942), p.122
41. THE MAKERS (1943), p.129
42. AERIAL RECONNAISSANCE (1943), p.132
43. WAR CAT (1943), p.135
44. TARGET AREA (1944), p.140
45. AENEAS AT THE COURT OF ĐIDO (1945), p.145
46. ST. BERNARD'S HYMN TO THE BLESSED VIRGIN (1949), p.149
47. TORQUATO TASSO TO THE CATS OF ST. ANNE'S (1952), p.151
48. AS YEARS COME IN AND YEARS GO OUT (1953), p.152
49. FOR AN EVENING SERVICE (1953), p.153
50. THE COSMOGRAPHERS (1957), p.154
51. FOR TIMOTHY, IN THE COINHERENCE (1973), p.156

THE POEMS

♣

In January 1898, Dorothy L. Sayers, approaching five years of age, moved with her parents from her birthplace in Oxford to a rectory in the parish of Bluntisham-cum-Earith in the Fen country. She dwelt there, taught by her parents and by governesses in French and German, until she departed for Godolphin School in Salisbury in January 1909.

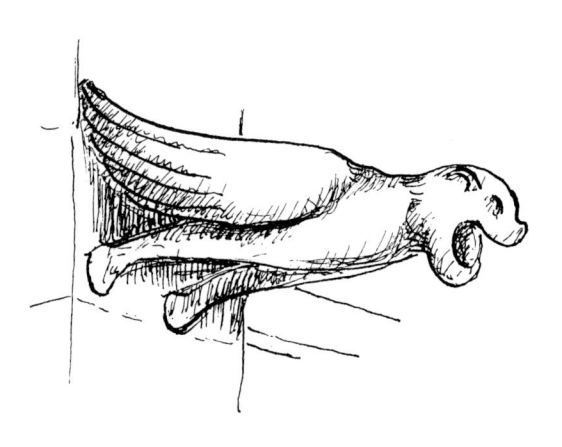

1.
THE GARGOYLE (1908 ?)

The Gargoyle takes his giddy perch
On a cathedral or a church.
There, mid ecclesiastic style
He smiles an early Gothic smile
5 And while the parson, full of pride,
Spouts at his weary flock inside,
The Gargoyle, from his lofty seat,
Spouts at the people in the street;
And like the parson, seems to say,
10 In accents doleful, 'Let us pray'.
I like the gargoyle best. He plays
So cheerfully on rainy days –
While parsons, no one can deny,
Are awful dampers when they're dry.

This poem was first published in Brabazon (p. 20) with the comment "This poem is undated. But it was probably composed some time in her mid-teens.... Neat, witty, with a pleasant acidity...."

Dorothy L. Sayers attended Godolphin School in Salisbury, Wiltshire, during the years 1909-1911. She was an outstanding student, active in dramatics and in debate, a pianist, a violinist, a sub-librarian for the modern language library, an editor of the school magazine *The Godolphin Gazette*, and winner of the Gilchrist Scholarship in Modern Languages at Somerville College, Oxford, 1912.

2.
TO SIR ERNEST SHACKLETON AND HIS BRAVE COMPANIONS (1910)

Who shall dare say that England's might is waning,
    And that her foes shall rule the seas instead of her,
    Because no more heroic sons are bred of her?
The story of these men who, uncomplaining,
(5) Endured such toil, her greater glory gaining,
    Excels it not all tales we ever read of her?
    Never again let the foul lie be said of her!
Mother of men, thy strength is still remaining.

And some for rich reward have sailed the seas
(10) For gold and fertile conquest, and laid down
At England's feet their gifts of gold; but these
Braving all perils, counting not the cost,
Hazarding all, deemed the whole world well lost,
    So they might add one laurel to her crown.

On 11 October 1910, the school went to County Hall in Salisbury to hear Sir Ernest Shackleton lecture on the topic "Nearest the South Pole." *The Godolphin Gazette* reported that the lecture "was an inspiring tale of British pluck and dogged endurance, told in the quietest manner, and all the more impressive on that account." The Sayers Petrarchan sonnet appears on page 21 of *The Gazette*, No. 44, Autumn Term, 1910. Barbara Reynolds notes that Dorothy sent a copy of the sonnet to Sir Ernest and received a reply from him "which she duly [copied] out in a letter to her parents" (p. 33).

3.
CAPTIVO IGNOTO (1910)

What was thy name, O man? and what the fault
  That bound thee long ago in iron bands,
To crouch amid the darkness of the vault,
  Far from the friendly reach of helping hands?

[5]   Did greed of gold ensnare thee, or the hate
        Of those that love too fiercely? Didst thou fall
    Braving the proud oppression of the great?
        Or as a traitor, by the castle wall
    Slinking by night to let the foeman through?
[10]   Wast thou some priest, with tongue too bold in blame?
    Knight, noble, churl or bondman? false or true?
        We ne'er shall know; the night has hid thy name;
    Thou art forgotten through the flight of years –
    And yet – the stone we touch hath felt thy tears.

This Elizabethan (or Shakespearian) sonnet reflects an experience which occurred six days prior to the lecture of Sir Ernest Shackleton. "On Wednesday afternoon, October 5th, Miss Jones took the VI. and Special VI. Forms to Old Sarum instead of the usual history lesson in the morning," reported a fellow-pupil of Sayers in *The Godolphin Gazette*. Sayers herself wrote an explanatory epigraph before the poem: "During the recent excavations at Old Sarum a pit was discovered, containing two pairs of iron manacles, and close by the skeletons of several criminals, who had been executed and buried in unconsecrated ground." The poem appears on page 25 of *The Godolphin Gazette*, No. 44, Autumn Term, 1910. It was copied out for Catherine Godfrey after the Oxford years. It may be found in the collection *Poems to Real People* in the Rare Book Room of the William Allan Neilson Library of Smith College, Northampton, Massachusetts. Cited by permission.

From 11 October 1912 until Trinity Term 1915 Sayers was in residence at Somerville. She received Class 1 Honours in French and, of course, the Degree Course Certificate. She was awarded the degree itself in October 1920, when Oxford University first conferred degrees on women; she received the M.A. degree at the same time.

From 1916 to 1920, she taught at Hull High School for Girls, returned to Oxford to work as an editor for Basil Blackwell, and then for another year she served Eric Whelpton as a bi-lingual associate at L'Ecole des Roches, near Verneuil in Normandy.

4.
PEREDUR (1912)

All day I wander through the meads,
Or else at random range the wood
Where the tall pine-trees, rood on rood,
Stretch o'er the hill-side, dusk & brown
[5] With heather, that goes sloping down
To meet the river & the reeds.

I have brave sports when all alone:
I set me up a slender wand
A hundred steps from where I stand,
[10] And take my staff to fling at it –
I'm grown so cunning, I can hit
A flying sparrow with a stone.

And if my mother's goats should stray
I speed so swiftly on their track
[15] I over-run & drive them back;
And finding once two does dismayed
I gave them chase through briar & glade
And brought them in, the self-same way.

But that was long ago, when I
[20] Knew not the chase, & thought indeed
My mother's goats, by ill-hap freed,
Had lost their horns through running wild –
And when she heard the tale, she smiled,
But let me hunt them by & by.

[25] So when the autumn comes apace,
And days are short & evenings drear,
Through the dark mists we seek the deer,
Ride fetlock deep in the wet leaves,
Until the hunt, returning grieves
[30] That early night hath hid the chase.

> Then, when the shadows slowly fold
> In dusk embrace the woods & plain,
> And all we sit at home again,
> Such grimly tales my old nurse tells
> [35] Of ill hobgoblins, warlocks, spells,
> As make the very blood run cold,
>
> The while my mother sits & spins
> The goats' long fleece, & dyes the threads,
> And Dwan & Dwved shape the heads
> [40] Of their sharp arrows; Brut, my hound [,]
> Lays his great jowl along the ground,
> Dreaming the merry hunt begins.
>
> At night I watch the shining stars
> Peer through the branches of the pines,
> [45] Pass, like the herds, in ordered lines
> From east to west perpetually,
> Or watch the dark clouds enviously
> Fleck the white moon with sable bars.
>
> Or laid in winter by the fire,
> [50] While my dull henchmen sleep & snore,
> I hear the whirling tempest roar,
> And beat against the rough-hewn wall,
> And shake the rafters of the hall,
> Like some strong man in foiled desire.
>
> [55] So all my days by wood & moor
> I pass, until I seem to be
> A beast like these shy beasts I see
> (To me not shy, that know me one
> With them) – alone, yet not alone –
> [60] Evrawc's son, Childe Peredur.

And yet, meseems it was not so
Long years agone. I close my eyes
And see before them great walls rise
Built of grim stone, & not, like these,
[65] Of the round trunks of forest-trees
Plastered with mud 'gainst rain & snow.

Dimly I see my father's eyes,
Grey – & his grey beard; from his head
There floats down somewhat green & red –
[70] I seem to see his limbs & breast
Shining & hard, as he were drest
All in bright steel, in wondrous wise.

I think that cannot be, for why
Should man go clothed in iron? A child
[75] Has fancies oft-times strange & wild –
All in a dream – yet, when I think
Thereon, I seem upon the brink,
The very brink of memory.

Six brothers had I – they are dead.
[80] I know what death means now, although
Long time they strove I should not know,
Before I learned to hunt; one day
I found a little bird, that lay
Stark – it had died, my mother said.

[85] But all six brothers dead – strong men!
My father dead, – How could they die
So soon, so many? Nought comes nigh,
Here in the woods, that could slay me,
Save when some tempest-shaken tree
[90] Falls, or the fierce boar leaves his den.

But if I ask my mother how
This chanced, she weeps, but will not speak,
And I am sorry, kiss her cheek,
Promise I will not ask again
[95] Because the question brings such pain
To her still eyes & quiet brow.

Yet to my doubts & her alarms
I think sometimes I hold the key
In these strange words o'erheard by me,
[100] Spoke once by Dwnn: "Aye first in fight
"Stout blade, bold lance, a goodly knight,
"Had seen great giusts & feats of arms."

He spoke – & saw me, hushed his voice,
O'er shoulder glancing, & I made
[105] As though I had not heard – afraid
To ask the sense of what I heard,
But every strange, unmeaning word
Thrilled through me, made my heart rejoice;

Like the remembrance of a dream
[110] Almost forgotten when I rise,
Till some chance word brings memories
Of rich, mysterious pleasures, taken
In the dim realms of faery – shaken
And scattered with the morning beam –

[115] Nameless & formless pleasures, yet
Delightful to the mind – even so
I feel my heart & liver glow,
And all my pulses leap & dance –
"Had seen great giusts – stout blade – bold lance" –
[120] I wonder & cannot forget.

Something within me lies asleep,
Some heritage of my sire, that wakes
From slumber sometimes; & it makes
Me long to leave the hill & wood,
[125] Hunt something better than the brood
Of wolf or bear; it lies so deep

I hardly know that it is there, –
But surely man was made for more
Than just to chase the bear & boar, –
[130] Sure, when I pray, I am ashamed
To weary the high God, unblamed,
For such a little, worthless prayer.

Such little things there are to ask,
There is so little I can do –
[135] I say my Paternoster through
(He likes to hear it, Mother says),
I thank Him for good hunting days,
For the rich garner & full cask;

I pray Him then for fruitful land,
[140] That He will bless the flocks & herds,
And then I say some more good words
Such as He likes, & in the tongue
That is in Heaven spoke & sung –
Of course I cannot understand; –

[145] It must be angels' language, though, –
'Tis so like music, sweet & strong
And solemn – like the river's song,
Or songs of birds & winds & showers,
Not like this Cymric tongue of ours –
[150] "Benedicamus Domino."

>   I pray that God will keep me pure –
>   The words my mother taught end there;
>   But once I made a tiny prayer
>   All of my own: "Sweet Jesus, give
> [155] Thy child a larger life to live." –
>   Such is the prayer of Peredur.

This poem portrays only the naive early life of Peredur, stopping short of the "larger life" for which he prays and which is narrated in *The Mabinogion*, a collection of Welsh Arthurian tales published by Lady Charlotte Guest in 1838-1849. Sayers was probably acquainted with the Everyman Library edition of this work (London: Dent, 1906); the story of Peredur appears on pages 176-219. He is identified with Perceval. Note the Welsh names in lines 39, 60, and 100, and mention of *Cymric* in line 149.

The original poem is to be found in a Mutual Admiration Society notebook (so indicated on the recto of the front cover) dated 1912-1913, owned by the Marion E. Wade Center, Wheaton College, Wheaton, Illinois. Immediately following the last stanza appears the signature "D. L. Sayers / M[ichaelmas] T[erm]1912". The twenty-six six-line stanzas of octosyllabic verse are an effective example of Sayers's ability to sustain excellent narrative poetry.

The poem is cited by permission of the Wade Collection.

5.
THE HORN (1912/1913)

From the French of A. de Vigny

> I love the voice of the horn in the woods at the close of day,
> Whether it sound the lament of the faltering stag at bay,
> Or the hunter's last good-night, with its echo faint & soft,
> Borne from leaf to leaf by the wind, & whirled aloft.
>
> 5   How often alone in the night, while the forest about me slept,
> I have smiled to hear that voice, & still more often wept,
> For meseemed that the sounds were such as wondrously foretold,
> Long ages since, the deaths of the Paladins of old.

O mountains azure-veiled! O land of dear delight!
10   Ringed summits of Marboré! Frazona's rocky height!
Rivers that roll & roar when the toppling snows unfreeze,
Springs & streams & torrents of the towering Pyrenees!

O flower-decked, snow-capped peaks, where summer & winter meet,
Your high brows bound with ice, green meadows about your feet!
15   'Tis there I would sit & dream, while faint to my ears is borne
The melody solemn & sweet that rings from a distant horn.

Sometimes the wanderer late blows out its thin, clear note,
Thrilling the silent night with the blare of its brazen throat;
Measured & mellow in cadence it falls, & re-echoes, & swells,
20   Answered from near and afar by the tinkling sheep-fold bells.

And the timid doe will not now go hide her, but stays her leap,
And pricks a listening ear as she hangs on the edge of the steep,
While the plunging waterfall mingles its never-ending chant
As it thunders adown the crags, to the songs of dim romaunt.

25   Souls of the warriors dead, are ye returned once more?
Is it you that speak with the voice of the horn, bold knights of yore?
Roncevaux! Ronceveaux! in thy vale of gloom & dread
Doth the shade of the mighty Roland walk yet uncomforted?

His heroes were fallen around him, for never a one did flee,
30   He stood at Oliver's side, alone of his chivalry,
And the African's trembling host ringed him in upon every side:
"Yield, Roland, thine hour is come!" the Moorish chieftain cried;

"Thy peers are fallen & slain & buried the swift stream under."
But he roared with the voice of a lion: "When the mountains start asunder
35   And rush from their age-long base to roof my Paladins' grave,
Then, maybe, but not till then will I yield to thee, Moorish slave!"

But he answered, "Yield or die – for behold, they fall! they fall!"
And lo! as he spake, a rock rolled down from the mountain-wall,
It rolled & bounded & fell, & crashed in the deep ravine,
40 Splintering the pine-tree tops, & the white foam flew between.

"Gramercy, a path! a path!" quoth Roland, the fearless count;
And he rolled it on with his hand till it lay at the foot of the mount,
Then leapt like a giant & stood on the firm rock valiantly,
And the army watched & wavered before him, ready to flee.

45 In peaceful talk meanwhile the knights with Charlemayn,
Leaving the mountain-slopes, passed down into the plain,
Already they smiled to see, on the far horizon line,
Of Luz & of Argolès the distant waters shine.

There was joy in the host, & the minstrel made ready the string, tuned it truer
50 To ring to the praise of the willows that lean o'er the laughing Adour.
The shepherdess smiled on the soldiers; the wine that was poured to the stranger
Was the red wine & sparkling of France; so rode they careless of danger,

For Roland guarded the pass; but Turpin the archbishop, sitting
At ease on his fair black palfrey with housings of purple (befitting
55 Him who rode, & who carried the holy Relics before),
Lifted his hand & spake, & said to the Emperor:

"Lo! sire, how the welkin is red, ringed round & riven with flame –
Get you back, for this march is accurst, & who shall tempt God without blame ?
St. Denys our aid! full surely these lights are souls that have passed,
60 And are borne into Paradise in a fiery vapour & blast.

"Twice I saw the lightning flash – yea, & twice it darted again – "
When sudden the note of the horn came pealing over the plain;
Astonied the Emperor stood as he harked to the well-known sound,
And he checked his barb's proud pace, & he gazed behind & around,

65   "Heard ye that?" – "Yea so, my lord, 'tis the shepherd's voice, that shrills
(The prelate answered in haste) to call the herds from the hills –
Nought else – unless it may be that on some dim mountain-side,
The green dwarf Oberon holds speech with his elfin bride."

So the Emperor rides on his way, but his brow is brooding & black,
70   More sullen it is than the storm, more dark than the thunderous wrack
And his heart is filled with a dread fore-boding of treacheries, –
When the blast rings out & fades, re-echoes, & wails, & dies.

"Woe! woe! 'tis my nephew's horn! O horror! a blast of death!
For if Roland calls for help it is with his latest breath.
75   Back! back, my knights! turn back! ride over the mountains again!
Tremble once more at our tread, thou traitor soil of Spain!"

The day's last fading fires are sinking on Roncevaux
As the sweating horses stand on the height of the ridge; below
Fleeing well nigh out of sight, on the dusky edge of the world,
80   Of the false & faithless Moor the banners show unfurled.

"Turpin, dost thou see ought, far down in the torrent-bend?"
"I see two warriors lie, one dying, & one dead;
Beneath the mass of a tall black rock they are crushed & torn,
And one in his stiffening hand still grasps an ivory horn;
Twice he sounded the call as his soul from his lips took flight."
Christ! how sad is the voice of the horn in the woods by night!

An autograph copy of this poem is possessed by the Marion E. Wade Collection, Wheaton College, Wheaton, Illinois (Wade/MS-164). It appears in the notebook labelled "Mutual Admiration Society," the name of the select group of Somerville College friends with whom Sayers was closely associated. It contains three other items: a poem and a play (authors unidentified) and Sayers's "Peredur." The notebook is dated 1912-1913, and "The Horn" is immediately followed by the signature "D. L. Sayers." Cited by permission.

    Alfred de Vigny (1797-1863) was a Romantic poet and novelist. While serving in the military, he spent a period near the Pyrenees and the site of the legendary pass from Roncevaux. The poem was published in 1826. Noteworthy in the poem is the author's love of nature and of the medieval period. The poem is full of sensuous details. Sayers embraced Romanticism and was, indeed, attracted throughout her life to *The Song of Roland*, a translation of which she published in the last year of her life.

In line 8, *Paladins* = the Twelve Peers of Charlemagne's court; line 10, *Marboré, Frazona* = places in the region of the French Pyrenees; line 24, *romaunt* = (archaic) tale of chivalry; lines 27-85, summary of *The Song of Roland* (although in the version Sayers translated and published in 1957, Archbishop Turpin stayed with Roland and died at Roncevaux); line 50, *Adour* = a river in southwestern France; line 68, *the green dwarf Oberon* = apparently the same folklore figure whom we meet in *A Midsummer Night's Dream*, Auberon in French.

6.
TO H. P. A. (1914)

[T.-p. *decorated in red and blue*] To / H. P. A./
[Verso of T.-p.] With love & best wishes from / [decorative monogram of D and S] / Christmas 1914 – /
p. [6]ʳ [*in red ink*] I behold a vision of pale love

> Friend, at the sacring of the bread & wine,
>   Your name passed silently across my
>   prayer,
> As a stray traveller, in a foreign shrine,
>   Salutes the altar, almost unaware.
>
> Thereafter, in the night beside my bed,   [5]
>   I saw the phantom of pale love go by,
> With fettered feet, dim torch & hanging head,
>   Weeping for all his lost activity.

p. [6]ᵛ [*in red ink*] that has survived his use;

"Behold, I was the servitor of Fame,"
  Said he, "& have outlived him, &
    men say   [10]
That now I should put out my useless flame,
  And die, & into nothing creep away.

"Ah! woe is me, immortal! doomed to live
  Fruitless, stumbling under Shame's chill
    yoke,
My wine of sacrifice poured through a sieve, [15]
  And my red Torch burnt out in soot & smoke.

p. [7]^r [*in red ink*] I ask: Is love then worthless, like barley

  "So poor I am & naked, I must bend
    Chidden, & cover my eternal face,
  Nor dare to speak the sweet name of
      my friend
  Except with laughter in my holy place." [20]

I said to God, "'Tis done, which was to do;
  Idle in furrowed field the plough-share
    stands,
And soon from ridge to ridge sprayed
    white with snow
  Stalks winter, with his chains between
    his hands;

p. [7]^v [*in red ink*] sown in a crop of wheat, or flowers that die

  "But he that sowed along the autumn soil [25]
    Cast in the barley with the wheat, unsought,
  And of that second harvest of his toil
    Shall he reap nought, O Lord, shall
      he reap nought?

"A vision of sad islands in the sea,
  Where summer upon summer unperceived [30]
Fades with its flowers & gem-bright
    colibri,
And trees twined hugely, marvellously
    leaved.

p. [8]^r [*in red ink*] unseen! My soul answers; it is not so

> "For when the field is sown for wheaten bread,
>> Of thy brown barley, none hath any need,
> I will burn love for stubble, Lord, I said, [35]
>> Thus planted, watered, waited, run to seed."

> Yet, for the throng beside the holy lake
>> Five barley loaves were made a feast
>>> divine,
> And, so the priest be there to bless & break,
>> Black bread & verjuice still are bread
>>> & wine. [40]

p. [8]^v [*in red ink*] and likens my friend to a

> As in a distant country a rich king
>> Once gave command to cast a brazen bell,
> And hang so high that men might hear it ring
>> Through all that land, & out to sea as well.

> Whereof in a short space, one man was bold [45]
>> To swear accomplishment, the price being
>>> set
> At fifty thousand talents of pure gold
>> Of royal mintage, measured out by
>>> weight.

p. [9]^r [*in red ink*] bell-founder, that toiled steadfastly

> Dawn upon dawn the clouds seemed red
>> for rain,
> Or at high noon fled blackly through
>> the south; [50]
> Night after night, the sky glowed red
>> again,
> Where the wide furnace stretched its
>> yawning mouth.

Each hour the founder toiled with hand &
        mind;
  But every night his soul deliciously,
With disembodied feet & unconfined, [55]
  Sought a steep place beside the
        glass-green sea.

p. [9]^v[*in red ink*] at the fashioning of a bell,

With folded arms 'twixt earth & heaven he
        stood,
  And the loud breakers sprayed his
        knees with salt,
Above, the Swan, like a five-jewelled rood,
  Swung in the fragrant dimness of the vault, [60]

Seaward, like lamps, he saw the lanterns ride
  Of anchored ships; & all the while his ear
Felt the slow shock & gigantic stride
  Of deep notes shake the silence far &
        near.

p. [10]^r[*in red ink*] which when it was made stood

Now, after weeks of toil, the broken mould [65]
  Brought the bell forth, true, with no
        stain nor flaw,
Where through the bronze ran the rich
        blush of gold,
And round about the mouth of it men
        saw

The heavenly judge in His appalling glory,
  And Christ upon the cross, & under both: [70]
"Amore et cruore non pavore
  Salvati nos, Ter-Sancte Sabaoth."

p. [10]^V [*in red ink*] in need of a tower to hang it in;

> And so the first part of the task was o'er,
>> But while the founder smiled to think
>>> thereon
> His soul leaned swiftly from him to the
>> shore, [75]
>> And while the tired body slept, was gone.

> On that dream-cliff rose now a mighty shape,
>> Four-sided granite, casement-pierced
>>> & high,
> There, sounding over seas from cape to cape,
>> The bell rushed to & fro melodiously. [80]

p. [11]^r [*in red ink*] for which cause he built a tower

> Thenceforth, while all the onerous seasons
>> turned,
>> Month on slow month beheld its courses
>>> rise.
> 'Mid throngs of stooping masons moved &
>> burned
>> The founder's fierce white face &
>>> eager eyes.

> High on the scaffold o'er the mounting wall; – [85]
>> No stone was set within its place unproved,
> He spared not vigil, craft, nor sweat at all
>> To build a dwelling for the thing he loved.

p.[11]^V [*in red ink*] To bear up the bell and

> In the deep rock 'twas rooted steadfastly,
>> That all the roughest winds which shake
>>> the town, [90]
> And beat the reeling war-ships back to
>> sea,
>> Should never bring the loud bell
>>> clamouring down.

Thence like a slender lily-stalk it sprung,
    That grows & stretches passionately, to
        bear
Its precious blossom with the golden tongue, [95]
    Tremulously a-sway in the quick air.

p. [12]^r [*in red ink*] cause its sound to be heard;

And all its sides were fretted &
        pierced through
With wonderful carved windows, gates
        of sound,
Until a morning cobweb strung with dew
    Seemed thicker; & a winding stair clung [100]
        round

Within, from floor to floor, & it was made
    Of hammered iron most intricately
        wrought,
That craftsmen might climb swiftly by
        its aid
To serve the bell, if e'er it needed
        aught.

p. [12]^v [*in red ink*] the tower now being finished & the

Sharp scythe of dawn, set swinging through
        the sky [105]
    To mow away long swathes of the night,
Strike on that virgin turret, lifted high
    Through lucent seas of waveless
        chrysolite.

Wreathe up her bridal forehead with fresh
        flowers
    Of mist; this is the day her lord will come, [110]
And scaling the wide stairways of her
        bowers,
    Set him within her citadel at home.

p. [13]^r [*in red ink*] bell hung up therein. The music

> Strike on her baron in his panoply
> > Of brazen armour, radiantly borne,
> A splendour of white sunrise on the sea, [115]
> > A glory of a long expected morn!
>
> Strike on the master-builder, fire with fire
> > Akin; smite flame upon his toil-
> > > worn hands,
> Flame on his face turned upward to
> > the spire,
> Since where his spirit stood, his body
> > stands [120]

p. [13]^v [*in red ink*] was everywhere heard; nevertheless the

> Fronting the day, while from the topmost
> > storey
> > The rich sound drips like sweetness
> > > from the comb:
> "Amore et cruore, non pavore" –
> > And slides & springs in music o'er the
> > foam.
>
> The tall king sat beside the tables spread, [125]
> > The candles flared at close of festival,
> The naked sunshine frowned upon his head,
> > When that first note came pealing
> > up the hall.

p. [14]^r [*in red ink*] tower found yet more favour than the bell

> Then he took horse, & rode toward the rock
> > Content; but when he saw that pride
> > > of stone, [130]
> And saw the unsleeping arches interlock,
> > And all the slender strength the sun
> > > shone on,

> He clipped the builder to him, crying:
> > "Behold,
> > This bell that thou hast made for me is
> > > worth
> > A very heavy price of minted gold, – [135]
> > > The tower is the eighth wonder of the
> > > > earth."

p. [14]^V [*in red ink*] to the astonishment of the master-builder.

> > So brought him in, & set at his right hand
> > > And clothed him on with robes of
> > > > richest price,
> > And yet the builder might not understand,
> > > But said: He could not build it
> > > > otherwise. [140]
>
> > So men make deathless things they know not
> > > of,
> > And you that work another prize to win,
> > > Still fashion for yourself a tower of love,
> > > > With my love set as a small stone therein.

p. [15]^r [*in red ink*] thus it is a great thing to be beloved;

> > And Love need take no shame for foolishness, [145]
> > > Nor seek to beat his useless torches out;
> > Our joys are winged prayers that straitly
> > > > press
> > > > Through mists of space & time to stand about
>
> > The awful stream which parts the quick &
> > > > dead;
> > > And, Master-builder, verily I think [150]
> > Our little loves shall stand you in good
> > > > stead
> > > When your pale feet pause at the bitter
> > > > brink.

p. [15]ᵛ[*in red ink*] and helpful at a man's latter end;

> And God will stoop out of His golden chair
> > And ask: "Who comes with such a noise of laughter,
> Whom the strong sea-birds on their wings do bear [155]
> > Over the flood, with songs before & after?"

> God keep you. – I have set you in your place,
> > Among the holy streets of this grey town;
> On you & us the pleasant gargoyle face
> > Of Oxford imperturbably looks down. [160]

p. [16]ʳ[*in red ink*] and for this cause I have made this poem.

> And she is like that chapel reredos rich
> > In carved quaint figures – yours among the rest;
> I choose to set a rose within your niche
> > Despite the verger.
> > > Ite, missa est.

"H. P. A." refers to Dr. Hugh Percival Allen, organist at New College and director of the Oxford Bach Choir. Why this attractively hand-done work of thirty-two pages did not reach him at Christmas 1914 (as the text designed) is interesting to ponder. Perhaps it was that Sayers may have considered it excessively personal and even a little erotic. (It must be remembered that Dorothy L. Sayers's "unconcealed passion" for Dr. Allen – to use Vera Brittain's phrase – was common knowledge in Somerville College. Sayers portrayed Dr. Allen in the 1915 Somerville Going-Down Play.) The poem contains esoteric material, presumably elements of conversation between Allen and Sayers. This copy may have been the one sent by the author to Mrs. K. I. R. Molyneux "as a Christmas present – with a really charmingly illuminated cover". (Mrs. Molyneux played violin in Allen's orchestra, and, like Sayers, was a great admirer of the Bach Choir Director.) The copy of the poem is now in the possession of the Bodleian Library and is cited by permission. Another autograph copy was sent to Catherine Godfrey: it contains the title "To Hugh Percy Allen" and has three additional stanzas at the beginning of the poem. The Godfrey copy is in the collection entitled "Poems to Real

People" now possessed by the Rare Book Room of the William Allan Neilson Library of Smith College, Northampton, Massachusetts; the three additional stanzas appear at the end of these remarks and are cited by permission. The Archives of the Dorothy L. Sayers Society contain two snippets from this poem, the poem-within-a-poem constituted by the rubrics heading the successive pages of the poem, and fourteen lines from various parts of the main poem itself.

> God was making a man one day
> In a kind of merry mood,
> And Heaven & Hell were there at play,
> And He asked them what they would.
>
> Gabriel asked for a strong staff;
> Raphael for a lyre;
> Satan wanted a hearty laugh,
> Tall Michael a sharp fire.
>
> Up rose Mary mild
> And kissed the man's eyes,
> And gave him the heart of a little child: –
> So it was on this wise.

The Marion E. Wade Center of Wheaton College, Wheaton, Illinois, has an autograph copy of this poem in a collection "Poems: 1914-1915" (Wade MS-167). It is dated 7 June 1914, and there is internal evidence that most of the rubrics were designed in this copy.

Colibri (l. 31) is an archaic word for a variety of humming-bird; *Five barley loaves* (l. 38) refers to the account in Scripture of the feeding of the multitude by Christ; see St. John vi.9; *Swan* (l. 59) is the same as *Cygnus*, a constellation in the Northern Hemisphere; *Amore et cruore non pavore / Salvati nos, Ter-sancte Sabaoth* (ll. 71, 72, 123), Latin, meaning "By love and by the blood are we saved, and not by fear, O thrice-holy God of hosts." (See the second epigraph of "The Drunkard," in *Catholic Tales and Christian Songs.*); *Chrysolite* (l. 108) is a variety of olivine, a magnesium iron sulphate, usually olive-green; *Ite, missa est* (l. 164) is a dismissing direction, given at the completion of the Mass.

Somerville College, Oxford.

7.
TO A LEADER OF MEN (1915)

CAPTAIN, if your strong bow should break in your hand,
    What shall we do in the terrible days?
"He at least," we said, "is sure to withstand;
    We shall take fire at the flame of his face
[5]   Though our vigil endure until morning, through weariness,
    doubt or disgrace."

Remember, the weak are pitiless for the strong,
    Whose backs are broad for the double share;
What! *your* eyelids are heavy? *You* find the night long?
    You have your moments of black despair?
[10] Never! your task is the bearing of burdens; go on, then,
    and bear.

Captain, if your strong heart should break with the load,
    We will be generous over your dust,
Forgive you for being a man when we thought you a god –
    Only sigh for our squandered trust –
[15] Have mercy on all strong men, most merciful Lord, and
    just!

This poem was the first poem Sayers published after she began her Oxford studies in Modern Languages at Somerville College, 1912. It appeared in *The Oxford Magazine*, 5 February 1915, p. 174, signed by the initials only "D. L. S." The poem also appears in *Unique Manuscript Magazine*, 1916, pp. 49-50. The latter is in the possession of the Bodleian Library, Oxford (MS. Eng. misc. e. 742).

As a war poem, this effort expresses Sayers's satire of the tradition that the poet must encourage the warrior in his duty.

She saw that her parents received a copy of this poem. She was perplexed that her father found it "amusing." "It is intended," she wrote to her parents on 14 February 1915, "to be immediately touching, and the last verse is grimly ironical." In the same letter she mentions Mrs. Molyneux (see Annotation of "To H. P. A." above), evincing some latent competitiveness with the lady (who also happened to be an outspoken admirer of Dr. Allen):

Mrs. Molyneux, who made the original remark which was the basis of the second verse – and in fact, of the whole thing, was struck dumb when she read it – being surprised to see an accident of our daily life come out into such a fine lyric!

8.

TO MEMBERS OF THE BACH CHOIR ON ACTIVE SERVICE (1915)

Now and again, o' Monday nights,
Do you see the little bicycle lights
Twinkling by two, and three, and four?
Do you see the open Museum door,
[5] And the fire-hose coiled on the dusty floor?

Stuck waist-deep in a slimy trench,
Your nostrils filled with the battle-stench,
Reek of powder and smoke of shell,
And poison fumes blowing straight from hell –
[10] Do your senses ache for another smell?

For the smell of fossils and sticks and stones,
Camphor and mummies and old dry bones,
Of strenuous singers, and gas and heat –
While you strove for a tone that was pure and sweet
[15] In air you could cut with a baton's beat?

When the guns are dumb and the shouting still –
Do you remember the pulses' thrill
When the loud voice leapt to a strong behest –
O you that sang with so brave a zest:
[20] *"Et iterum venturus est"?*

Maybe you've forgotten us; small your blame
If we should forget you, foul our shame,
Though on Monday nights, as in days bygone,
Tenor with alto hurries on
[25] Past the bones of the iguanadon.

>   From singer to singer the space is wide
>   Where knee pressed knee once, side pressed side,
>   And through every fugue that ripples and runs,
>   And through every chorus that smites and stuns,
> [30] There breaks the crash of your distant guns.
>
>   Howbeit, of this I am full fain,
>   That the quick and the dead shall come again,
>   And all together, I dare to guess,
>   Sing Bach in Heaven – or Heaven were less
> [35] Than this poor earth in mirthfulness.

This poem, competently unified in its theme, adroitly balanced in diction and tone, was published in *The Oxford Magazine*, Volume XXXIV, No. 12 (18 February 1916), p. 194. It had been included among the manuscript poems sent by Sayers to Miss Rowe in 1915, is now in the Bodleian Library, Oxford.

The Latin quotation from Bach (line 20) means "And [when] he shall have come again;" it appears in the Latin version of the Nicene Creed and was used in the Bach *B Minor Mass* "Credo." Christopher Dean has reminded me that in Chapter V of *Whose Body?* Lord Peter is heard singing "et iterum venturus est."

The Marion E. Wade Center, Wheaton College, Wheaton, Illinois, has an autograph manuscript copy of this poem – possibly the original – in "Poems: 1914-1915" (Wade/MS-167).

Barbara Reynolds notes in her biography of Sayers (p. 74) that Muriel Jaeger wrote to tell her that Dr. Allen had laid down his baton in the middle of a rehearsal and in poignant tones had urged the Choir to read the poem.

During Sayers's Oxford days, the Bach Choir met on Monday nights in the University Museum, devoted to the natural sciences. Hence (line 25), the *iguanadon* = large herbivorous dinosaur.

9.
ICARUS (1916)

(From the French of Ph. Desportes, 1545-1606.)

HERE fell young Icarus, that dared to climb
    Heaven, and, audacious, cleave the starry plain;
    Here dropped his wingless body; hearts remain
All envy at a failure thus sublime.
[5]   O happy labour of a glorious prime,
        Winning such vantage from so small a pain!
        Happy mishap, so greatly filled with gain
It leaves the vanquished victor over time!

To daunt his youth, no untried paths availed,
[10]   His strength it was, and not his spirit, failed;
        None save the prince of stars might seal his doom;
He died while bound on high adventure's quest;
All heaven was his desire, the sea his rest;
    Where were a loftier aim, or statelier tomb?

This very accomplished translation of a Petrarchan sonnet was published in *The Oxford Magazine*, XXXIV, No. 17 (5 May 1916), p. 286. Philippe Desportes (1546-1606) was a disciple of the *Pléiade*.

10.
THOMAS ANGULO'S "DEATH" (1916)

Señor, your health! This ranting dries the mouth.
Ah! that's the rare, ripe stuff. Your honour's choice?
Your honour knows the house? – I thought as much!
For the tried palate, the rich, cobwebby
[5]   Far corner bin – for the casual God-knows-whom
Grapeskins and water. Trade, sir, trade! – And now
How did you like our play – Eh? – Well, consider!
I had brave thoughts of classic excellence
In the old days, but now I'm glad enough
[10]   To get my living vulgarly, cry out
A truce with Aristotle, – eat, drink, laugh –

That's as much as a man can aim at nowadays.
And for this turn I've laughed my bellyful.
Think of it, sir: our tumbril – Michael here,
[15] That plays Old Nick, squats driving, tail a-cock –
I with my skull-face, Andrea, winged and crowned,
The wench, our cloth-of-tinsel empress – all
Our motley – creak, creak, jangle-jang, crack whip,
Bladder and bells. – When up there starts a thing –
[20] 'Faith, sir, I thought the gruff old jester, Death,
Had ambled up on his pale bag o' bones
To see what sort of show I made of him!
A great, thin, scarecrow, rotten-armoured rogue –
A very ambulant anatomy . . . .

[The player, a fellow of some pretentions to gentility and education, would here have narrated the details of Don Quixote's conversation, and of his unfortunate adventure with the Fool. His own opinion is that the poor knight was mad, but he adds:]

[25]   There was
A simpleness about him, and a zest;
I think he lived his piteous mummery
More merrily, that this was real to him,
And his defeats, right bruises, stiff and sore,
[30] Not painted, like our Christ's in the miracles.
You've known what dreaming is. I left my home,
The schools, my fortune, to bedaub my face
And mouth out a few gagged and garbled lines
Of villainous metre; sacrificed, attained –
[35] Yet somehow, I have lost the soul o' the thing;
A man can't snuff the early morning scent
Of the young violets, while he carries them
To market – he's got used to it. So we.
The pity is, we grow professional
[40] And live outside ourselves. But, sir, to play
And keep the glamour! Wear the gilded wings
And verily believe one's self an angel!
That were a thing worth doing.
                         And a thing
[45] A man can only do by being mad,
Or so I gather.

OP. I.

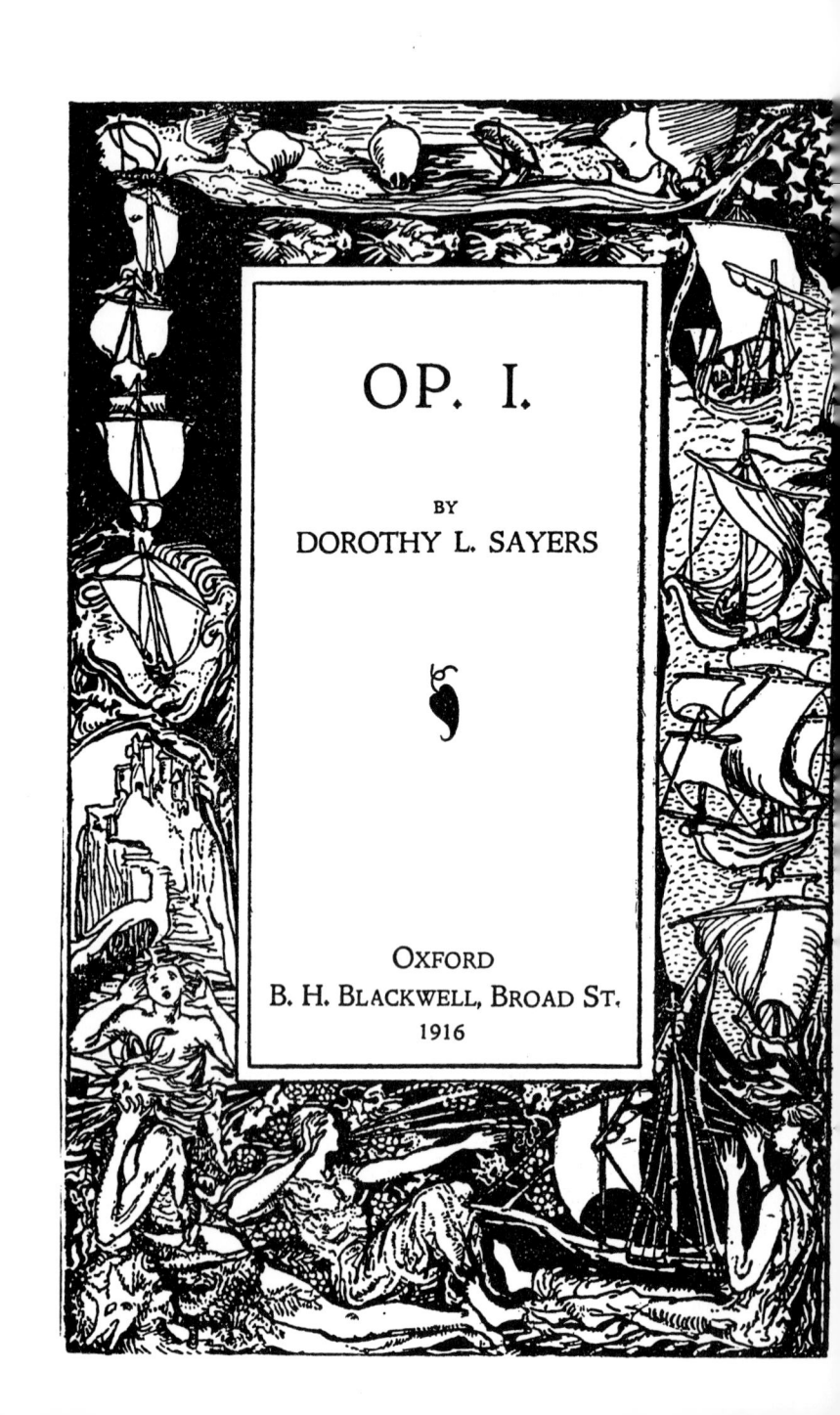

BY
DOROTHY L. SAYERS

OXFORD
B. H. BLACKWELL, BROAD ST.
1916

> And, indeed, I felt
> No rag of pity for the fellow – laughed
> To split my sides. . . .
[50]   I fear I'm talking, sir,
> And you'd be moving; pray you, pardon me;
> God keep you, sir – a thousand thanks! Good-day.

Labelled "THE PRIZE FRAGMENT. / FRAGMENTS OF AN UNPUBLISHED POEM BY ROBERT/BROWNING." The editor of *The Saturday Westminster Gazette* for 20 May 1916, p. 9, offered these comments: "Our prize is awarded to H. P. RALLENTANDO for a spirited treatment of an incident which Browning might easily have chosen for such a monologue as the one outlined" (p. 8); and "[This poem seems to have been inspired by the reading of 'Don Quixote,' Part II, Ch. XI., and was apparently intended for inclusion in 'Men and Women.' Only the opening and concluding passages are written, but a few notes in the poet's handwriting sufficiently indicate the course which the monologue would have taken.]" (p. 9) Sayers used as pseudonym for this poem, which brilliantly displays her acquaintance with Robert Browning's dramatic monologues, the thinly-disguised name of her idol, Dr. Hugh Percival Allen, in the form she employed in the 1915 Somerville Going-Down Play: H. P. RALLENTANDO.

OP. I was the first book published by Dorothy L. Sayers. It was printed for B. H. Blackwell in Oxford to appear before the end of the year 1916 as Number 9 in the series ADVENTURERS ALL, "A Series of Young Poets Unknown to Fame," but it was not available until 7 January 1917. The number of copies printed was 350. Other poets in the ADVENTURERS ALL series had included Wilfrid Rowland Childe, Elizabeth Rendall, Esther Lilian Duff, T. W. Earp, Frank Betts, Sherard Vines, Aldous Huxley, and Stephen Reid-Heymann.

The title of this book and, as well, the first prefatory poem suggest a first *opus*. Three of the poems ("Hymn in Contemplation of Sudden Death," "Epitaph for a Young Musician," and "Matter of Brittany") had been published elsewhere earlier. Two of the poems ("A Man Greatly Gifted" and "The Elder Knight") were reprinted in *Songs for Sale: An Anthology of Recent Poetry*, ed. E. B. C. Jones (Oxford: B. H. Blackwell, 1918), pages 38-42.

II.
LAY (1916)

"Item, quant est des laiz, c'est une chose longue et malaisee a faire et trouver, car il y faut avoir xii. couples, chascune partie en deux, qui font xxiiii. Et est la couple aucunefoiz de viii vers, qui font xvi.; aucunefoiz de ix. qui font xviii.; aucunefoiz de x. qui font xx.; aucunefoiz de xii qui font xxiiii., de vers entiers ou de vers coppez. Et convient que la taille de chascune couple a deux paragrafes soient d'une rime toutes differens l'une a l'autre, excepte tant seulement que la darreniere couple des xii., qui font xxiiii., et qui est et doit estre conclusion du lay, soit de pareille rime, et d'autant de vers, san redite, comme la premiere couple."

Eustache Deschamps: L'Art de Dictier

I

MUMMERS! let love go by
    With his crown upon his head,
Beaten royally
    Of gold, heavy and red;
[5]   Your tinsel garments fly
    To the trip of a lightsome tread,
    The gusty gale has fled,
And your garlands are blown awry.

Sniggering, whisperingly,
[10]   What was the thing you said?
"Poor old love? Oh, ay!
    Put him away to bed
With his wearisome song and sigh –
    We've a ragtime tune instead." –
[15]   But yours is already dead,
    And his can never die.

II

Oxford! suffer it once again that another should do thee wrong,
I also, I above all, should set thee into a song;
    I that am twice thy child have known thee, worshipped thee, loved thee, cried
[20]   Thy name aloud to the silence and could not be satisfied,
    For my hands were stretched to clutch thee, draw thee up to my side,
And my heart has leapt and my breath has failed, to hear the tongue
    Of Tom toll in the dark, and straight unpanoplied
    My soul has almost died.

[25] Bear with me as thou hast borne with all thy passionate throng
Of lovers, the fools of love; for the great flood sweeps along
    From the hills into the sea, and all their boats go down with the tide;
    And thou shalt stand unmoved, when the wreck of the world beside,
    When the loveless cities of greed slip down in their ruined pride
[30] And crumble into the gulf of Time. Thou shalt be strong
    With Thebes and On and Memphis, where the deathless gods abide,
A city sanctified.

III

    If I shall sing of thee in antique rime,
      Stately and cold as moons that near eclipse,
[35]   And intricate as bells rung down in time,
      It is to keep the madness from my lips,
      Whereby the lover's tongue stumbles and trips,
    Uttering foolishness, and thy sublime
      White brow is marred with mockery – garlands to whips,
[40]   Sceptres to reeds are turned, and worship to a crime.

> Think, magic city, that as each dear chime
>   Thrills the mute, friendless night, or stealthily drips
> Through all the noise of noon from prime to prime,
>   Continually some new soul comes to grips
>   With thee and all the power of thee. He slips
> To seaward, weighs out anchor from the slime,
>   Following the wake of countless golden ships,
> Thy figure at the prow, to some far western clime.

IV

> Thou art so magical
>   Thou makest me afraid,
> Lest some great bolt of desolation fall,
>   And thou in dust be laid
> With Babylon and Nineveh the tall;
> Or some enchanted lake will cover thee all,
>   And through quadrangle, cloister, colonnade,
> Four-coloured fishes swim, and, faint and small,
> Up through the waves at midnight the bells of Magdalen call.
> Through midnight waters mighty Tom will call.

> Or when, perchance, the pall
>   Of some nocturnal shade
> Unstarred, more dewy-dark than usual,
>   Lifts upon hill and glade,
> I fear lest sunrise strike upon no wall,
> No winding street nor ghost-white pinnacle –
>   Only on level woodlands, lonely made
> Of thee, as once, by arts incredible,
> The holy castle vanished behind Sir Percival,
> At morning light was not, for Percival.

V

    Once Nimue, the lady of the lake,
        Wound aged Merlin in the coils of sleep,
        And cast the silence of the luminous, deep
    Green forest all about him, there to take
    His rest for ever; no alarm might shake
        The stillness, no wild creature snuff or peep
        On him, no knight arouse him with the leap
    Of his tall war-horse plunging through the brake.

    And that enchantress, Venus, for the sake
        Of young Pygmalion, weary to see him creep
        Kissing his idol's senseless foot, and weep,
    Smote life into the stone, and so did slake
    His thirst of love. And thou? The willows quake
        By the clear Cher, thick-clustered dewdrops steep
        The heads of mossy gargoyle-beasts, that keep
    Their wide, shy smile. Age dreams and young men wake.

VI

    Only one painter could have painted thee,
        Still mother with the unimpassioned eyes,
    Dark with the mystery
        Of many centuries,
        Couldst thou have walked in a woman's guise
        Under the blue, exulting skies
    Of Italy
        In the great sunrise.

    All things that were, and now are, and shall be
        Graven upon thy heart, have made thee wise
    To smile inscrutably;
        All aid thou couldst despise
        Of reeds and fanciful psalteries,
        Strange face of kindness and cruelties,
    Immutably
        Without surprise.

VII

Thy name is as the scent of things departed –
  Of myrrh and unremembered frankincense,
  Stored in the niches of dim chapels, dense
  With hidden tales of penitence,
With wreathed prayer and desperate vows red-hearted,
  Whose ancient eloquence
  Knocks on the doors of sense
  When in thy haunted shrines I kneel without
    defence;

Like one that sails on ice-dark waters, charted
  By wrinkled mariners at dear expense,
  Who trims the sails with careful diligence,
  And though the pole-star burn intense,
Shudders to know how many ships thus started,
  Feeling the wrath commence
  Of old experience,
  And drowned green ghosts that crawl from unsus-
    pected dens.

VIII

How shall I let thee go? for thou didst wring
  All myself from me; I would not withhold
One citadel, but gave thee everything.
  Perhaps a better wisdom had controlled
The gift, had kept some solitary string
  Thou couldst not shake, some secret still untold,
  So that thou hadst not left me unconsoled
At thy departure. All this sorrowing
  Would not be mine to-day had I been strong of old.

But now – too late! the fleeing shadows bring
  The unsheathed swords of morning, sharp and cold,
Thou breakest from me – I am weakening –
  Last night wast thou so mighty? I behold
Glimmering betwixt the feathers of thy wing,
  Westward the stars, eastward the sunrise gold,

O stay! my hands about thy feet are bold.
Curse me or bless, thou godlike, deadly thing,
   By the Lord's living face, I will not loose my hold!

IX

[135]   The moonlight over Radcliffe Square,
             Small sunset spires that drowse and dream,
         Thin bells that ring to evening prayer,
             Red willow-roots along the stream,
             And perilous grey streets, that teem
[140]   With light feet wandering unaware,
             And winter nights with lamps agleam,
         Globed golden in the violet air;

         Odd nightmare carven things, that stare
             Spell-stricken in a voiceless scream,
[145]   The worn steps of an ancient stair,
             With oaken balustrade and beam –
             Such things are weightier than they seem,
         These marks my branded soul must bear,
             Pledges that Time cannot redeem.
[150]   And yet God knows if I shall care!

X

         "Iseult! Iseult! day follows day
         With weary feet; the bitter spray
         Flies fitfully over the waterway.
             The gull's harsh crying
[155]   Is cruel as death. O far away
         Are the years when we made holiday;
         My hair and beard show very grey
             In the bed where I am lying.

         "All the wonderful songs of May,
[160]   Roundel, madrigal, virelay,
         I cannot remember them now to play,
             For yesternight I was trying

>   To bring them back, but the harp-strings fray,
>   And I only know that the songs were gay."
> [165]   Thus and thus did Sir Tristram say
>   In the hour that he was dying.

XI

>   They say the waters cannot drown
>   Love. I believe it. Set this down:
>   That I believed and uttered thus.
> [170]   Whatever things the years discrown,
>   Somehow, love, I would have it known
>   My youth was not ungenerous,
>   And I could kneel to kiss thy gown,
>   As every honest lover does.
>
> [175]   For when beneath the winter's frown
>   Forth to the forest goes the clown,
>   Whistling, when winds are blusterous,
>   To gather kindling for the town,
>   There on his faggots sere and brown
> [180]   A few dry leaves hang dolorous
>   In witness of the spring's renown –
>   And it is even so with us.

XII

>   I, even I,
>   Have loved in joy and dread.
> [185]   Now my spinning-wheel I ply
>   Like the peasant-girl, that wed
>   With a king (they say), and try
>   With hands and heart of lead
>   To spin out a golden thread
> [190]   From the dusty straws and dry.
>
>   I will not weep nor cry
> [195]   For work unperfected,
>   Still labouring faithfully
>   I have no tears to shed.

> For love goes harping high,
>   And is remembered,
>   Mummers! when you are sped
> With all the lips that lie.

This masterly handling of a very difficult verse form was first published in *Oxford Poetry 1915*, edited by G. D. H. Cole and T. W. Earp (Oxford: B. H. Blackwell, 1915), pp. 50-57. (This volume contains, besides poems by two other Somervillians [Agnes E. Murray and Dorothy H. Rowe], some of the earliest work of Aldous Huxley and J. R. R. Tolkien.)

The version here follows the reprint in *OP. I* (1916), pp. 20-31. The citation from Eustache Deschamps (c. 1346-c. 1406), in contrast to the version in *Oxford Poetry 1915*, lacks all accent marks. Barbara Reynolds has translated this citation concisely and clearly:

> As for the lay, it is a long affair and difficult to compose, for there must be 12 stanzas, each divided into 2, making 24 in all. The stanzas can consist of 8, 9, 10 or 12 lines (totalling 16, 18, 20 or 24 for the pair); and the lines may be of full length or short. The rhymes of each pair must be different, except for the last, the twelfth (which brings the total up to 24 divisions), which is and must be the conclusion of the lay. This must have the same rhyme and the same number of rhymes as the first pair, without a refrain. (Barbara Reynolds, *The Passionate Intellect* [Kent, Ohio: Kent State University Press, 1989], p. 238n.)

The intricate interweaving of lines and rhymes in this highly specialized poetic structure has been matched by Sayers's ingeniously inwrought pattern of ideas and images. This feature of the poem accords brilliantly with the visual design surrounding the title-page of *OP. I*: the intertwined banner of words from II Maccabees xv. 39 – "Speech finely framed delighteth the ears of them that read the story."

The theme of the work is that the place, purposes, and pursuits of Oxford ought to be revered because of the uniqueness of the coalescence of Oxford's history, tradition, and ideals. Magic and mystery supply apt images, among them Pygmalion, *La Gioconda*, and the biblical patriarch Jacob at Peniel.

The Marion E. Wade Center, Wheaton College, Wheaton, Illinois, has an autograph of this poem – possibly the original – in

"Poems: 1914-1915" (Wade/MS-167). It is followed by a one-page summary of the form of the poem: line-lengths, metres, and rhyme-schemes.

12.
THE LAST CASTLE (1916)

FRIENDS, have you found things changed, in very sooth,
    Since all we sat beside the silver streams,
And saw the sunshine of unhampered youth
    Bathe the green fields till they were white with dreams?
[5]   Why then, beware! for I will let the flood
Of memory burst its banks, and with no ruth
    Stir up once more the glamour in your blood,
Break through and bear away the bonds of truth.

The roads of life wind onward through the plain;
[10]   Youth is Knight Percivale, the hero-fool;
The spell-bound lad, that thinks himself in vain
    A world-wise man, being yet a boy at school;
    He nightly in strange castles comes to lie,
And there, all wonder – of wisdom not one grain –
[15]   Lets pass the Holy Graal unquestioned by,
Through weary years to be desired again.

O that last faery castle, where we met,
    And dwelt three years together, you and I!
There was in her no sorrow, no regret
[20]   But faded to a purple pageantry,
    Joy was a lamp, and love a faint perfume –
Her spires were full of secrets; fairer yet
    Was every bower, and each enchanted room
When with mysterious rains her courts were wet.

* * * * * * *

[25]   To the last banquet of the appointed days
         We came; there was no change; I drew my chair
       With heedless hands up to my usual place;
         Though afterwards, a strangeness stirred my hair
         To think that this was done for the last time;
[30]   From wizard windows died the sunset rays
         Aslant through jewelled figures of ancient rime,
       And down from the heaped beakers dropped the blaze.

       And those tall pillars, dim as amethyst,
         Soaring like smoke incredibly aloof,
[35]   Where, lift on high above the censer-mist,
         Pale capitals glimmered in the golden roof –
         O marvellously, magically went
       Our music up among them, coldly kissed
         From pipe and reed, or plucked in thin consent
[40]   By white, frail fingers of the lutenist.

       The spell-bound and unalterable years
         Were dying, and the windless night stood by,
       Her moon like candle-light, her stars like spears,
         At watch; the echo of our minstrelsy
[45]   Slid with a strange delight most pitiful
       Down the long line of slender, shadowy biers,
         Like breezes on the surface of a pool,
       Too slight to shake the dew of gossamers.

       Those songs of ours were so fantastical
[50]   They held faint presage of the time at hand,
       Though we knew well, this visionary hall
         Stood on the limits of our faery land,
         That it and all its treasures, howso rare,
         Must fade at sunrise with the watchman's call,
[55]   And we in iron harness forward fare,
       Departing from our dead youth's funeral.

                This was our singing: –

The First Song   *School of Oxford-cult*

WAR-TIME

The splendour of the year, no less
Is on thy loveliness,
The light in no less glory falls
[60]   On thy unchanging walls
Now, than in other days;
No sorrow can displace
The ordered beauty of thy face;
Yet thou dost watch the water-ways
[65]   For thy lost lovers, with a grave and panoplied distress;

Like Iseult looking over-sea
With wan face wearily
Under the coils of braided gold
Resplendent fold on fold.
[70]   And girded queenliwise
With jewels of rich price,
With vair, and scarlet of fine dyes,
But still with shadow-haunted eyes
Straining to Tristram hard bested in far-off Brittany.

The Second Song   *School of Paradox*

PIPES

[75]   I sat beside the river
         when the summer sun was bright,
And blew brave music
         as loudly as I might,
On the sweet, hollow Pan-pipes –
         they were my delight.

On the bare, black mountain
         where the storm had stripped the ground,
I breathed a broken melody
         quite softly; and I found
[80]   That all my pipes were shattered
         with the shrillness of the sound.

God keep the river
    and God keep the reeds –
I am for the City
    full of men's deeds,
To build a great organ
    for my new needs.

The Third Song *School of Religious Ornament*
CAROL
O know you how Queen Mary sits
[85]   In heaven's brightest bowers,
Tall lilies in her garden-beds,
    Set round with gilly-flowers?

And know you how Queen Mary sits
    With rings upon her hands,
[90]   While the seven blessed Virgins bind
    Her hair in golden bands?

And when the Lord will comfort her
    For her seven swords of pain,
He comes to stand beside her knee,
[95]   A little child again.

The Fourth Song *School of Strong Simplicity*
RECKONING
I said to the devil one day,
"What is the price that a man must pay?
What is the end of shameful desire?"
    He answered: "Hell-fire."

[100]   "You sell sin for a song," I said,
"And the day of reckoning is far ahead;"
Nor knew that, even when he threatens hell-fire,
    The devil is a liar.

For the bitter end of shame
[105]   Is not any sort of fire or flame,
But the chill of a scorn too sick for laughter,
    Here, not hereafter.

The Fifth Song　　　　　　　　　　　　　　　　　　*School of Sentiment*
WOMANLINESS

The Master of the house came and sat him down to dine,
And I served him on my bended knees with bread and meat and wine,
[110] With a peacock stuffed with peaches, in his pride for all to see,
And the name of that resplendent dish was "Golden Flattery."

I served him with the bread of Toil, with meat of Strength and Sense,
All on a fair white napkin of utter Reverence,
With every course I brought him a gay and gilded cup
[115] Where God's good wine of Laughter unceasing bubbled up.

And well I know the banquet was all the heart could wish,
For I served the Love I bore him as the salt with every dish,
As salt to the meat, and as savour to the wine
When my great Lord Paramount sat down to dine.

The Sixth Song　　　　　　　　　　　　　　　　　　*Pastoral School*
HARVEST

[120]　　As we walked through the merry, merry meads,
　　　　　　All in the month of May,
　　　'Twas you that wore the gown of green,
　　　　　　And I the gown of grey;
　　　For you I wept, for you I sighed,
[125]　　For you I very nearly died –
　　　　Hey, fol the diddle diddle day,
　　　　　　Hey, fol the dero day.

　　　But now as we come harvesting
　　　　　　When the leaves are growing old,
[130]　　It's you that wear the gown of grey
　　　　　　And I the gown of gold,
　　　For me you weep, for me you sigh,
　　　For me I think that you will die –
　　　　Hey, fol the diddle diddle day,
　　　　　　Hey, fol the dero day.

The Seventh Song   *School of Metrical Experiment*

SNAP-DRAGONS

I have the streets in mind
And the yellow sun, –
    Lad, you are left behind, –
    All that is done.

[140] Snap-dragons on the wall
Were homely to see, –
    What was it after all
    But vanity?

Snap-dragons on the wall
[145] In my garden too, –
    There is little to recall
    For me and you.

Dead blossoms adrift
Are falling away, –
[150]   You never gave me a gift
    Would last for a day.

Swift is darkness – swift
The death of a flower, –
I never gave you a gift
[155]   Would last for an hour.

Gone is the level light
From the wide lands, –
    I would be glad tonight
    Of the touch of your hands.

The Eighth Song   *School of Polite Letters*

SELF-DEFENCE

[160] My merry lord, I wonder when
I shall behold your face again.

Years hence – a month – a week, may be, –
How will you show yourself to me?

If high-enthroned and far away
I will recall our vanished day.

And work for you and worship you
In all things as I used to do.

But should I turn to find you near –
I'll have forgotten you, my dear!

The Ninth Song   *Pre-Raphaelite School*

SYMBOL

I found him in the church-yard,
    My brother who had died,
With white lilies above him,
    And a hemlock by his side.

Men plant the lilies
    In token of God's grace,
But the green and deadly hemlock,
    He grows in his own place.

With the sick lily-odour
    I was all faint within,
It was like a sweet and a seemly lie
    To cover the reek of sin.

And truth goes trim and decent
    In a rich man's funeral,
But rich men will turn rotten,
    And so shall we all.

Now the sour smell of the hemlock
    Is honest on the breath,
It is like the after-taste of sin,
    And the foretaste of death.

Thus was our singing.

When lo! betwixt the viol and the flute
    One struck a sudden and a haunting sound;
Each looked upon his neighbour and was mute,

          And let the myrtle branches fall to ground,
              Being afraid; for this was like the noise
[195]   Of something shifting nightly at the root
              Of a tall pleasure-house, whose airy poise
          Rests on the restless quicksand dissolute.

The Last Song

          The roadways of the blessed land
              Are set with poplar trees,
[200]   And when we ride beneath the morn
          The glad ears of the bearded corn
              Are brushed against our knees.

          Look long. To-morrow we shall stand
              Thronged in the dreadful street,
[205]   And bloody hands of men o'erborne
              Will clutch us by the feet.

          And the day broke, and there we stood forlorn
              Without the gates; a long and piercing blast
          Intolerable, came from the warder's horn,
[210]   The memory of all the years gone past,
              And blank as death the road behind us lay.
          So, while we gazed, we heard the heartless scorn
              Of ragged wanderers who thronged our way,
          Women and men, both wicked and way-worn.

The *OP. I* version of "The Last Castle" fills pages 32-46. The poem also exists in four manuscript copies. It was, first, among the items sent by Sayers to Miss Rowe in 1915; this manuscript is in the Bodleian Library, Oxford. The Rare Book Room of the William Allan Neilson Library of Smith College, Northampton, Massachusetts, possesses a second manuscript copy, the copy made by Sayers for Catherine Godfrey, also in 1915. The Rowe and Godfrey copies are identical in substance; only very minor variations in placement on a page, in punctuation, and in mechanics are present. A third manuscript copy was sent by Sayers to Muriel Jaeger at the end of July 1915; in an accompanying letter she referred to "the scoffing labels of the various 'schools' which we used to patronise."

The Marion E. Wade Collection, Wheaton College, Wheaton, Illinois, also has an autograph copy of this poem – possibly the original – in "Poems: 1914-1915" (Wade/MS-167); but the first twenty-four lines of the *OP. I* version are missing, and in their place are three lines from the last part of Section 4 of "Lay", above. (See *The Letters of Dorothy L Sayers*, ed. Reynolds, Hodder and Stoughton, 1993, Vol I, pp. 110-111.)

The Rowe copy has a note: "This is a poem for all us vain, sentimental, honest fools of M[utual] A[dmiration] S[ociety], & for any other such that have loved Oxford." This statement, of course, does not appear in *OP. I.*, which does, however, contain the lines from Section 4 of "Lay". The first three stanzas in the *OP. I* version are all new. Minor changes in spelling or diction also appear: *rime* for *rhyme* (l. 31); *above* for *beyond* (l. 36); *thin* for *their* (l. 39); *All on* for *All with* (l. 113).

The numbered song-titles and the designated schools undergo some changes in *OP. I*: "WAR-TIME" for "1914" in the first song; "*School of Religious Ornament*" replaces "Bread & Wine School" in the third song; "Hell-Fire School" in the fourth song becomes "*School of Strong Simplicity*"; the fifth title is altered from "Symbolico-Sentimental School" to "*School of Sentiment*"; there is an omission of ("Pantorim") under the title SNAP-DRAGONS in the seventh song.

13..
THE THREE KINGS (1916)

THE first king was very young,
   O balow, balow la lay,
With doleful ballads on his tongue,
   O balow, balow la lay,
[5]   He came bearing a branch of myrrh
Than which no gall is bitterer,
   O balow, balow la lay,
     Gifts for a baby King, O.

>   The second king was a man in prime,
> [10]   *O balow, balow la lay,*
>   The solemn priest of a solemn time,
>   *O balow, balow la lay,*
>   With eyes downcast and reverent feet
>   He brought his incense sad and sweet,
> [15]   *O balow, balow la lay,*
>   *Gifts for a baby King, O.*
>
>   The third king was very old,
>   *O balow, balow la lay,*
>   Both his hands were full of gold,
> [20]   *O balow, balow la lay,*
>   Many a gaud and glittering toy,
>   Baubles brave for a baby boy,
>   *O balow, balow la lay,*
>   *Gifts for a baby King, O.*

The Dorothy L. Sayers Society held an international competition for a musical setting of the poem "The Three Kings" to commemorate the centenary of the author's birth. Stephen Cleobury, the Director of Music at King's College, Cambridge, judged the competition, and the winning composer was Simon Hancock, whose setting was for a four-part choir.

The prize was awarded at a luncheon at King's College, Cambridge, on 24 November 1993 by Lord Runcie, former Archbishop of Canterbury and the present patron of the Sayers Society. The first performance of the Centenary Carol was at King's College, sung by members of King's and Trinity choirs. It was then sung at Canterbury Cathedral on Christmas Eve 1993 and broadcast on Classic fM on Christmas Day.

The poem appears on p. 54 of *OP. 1*.

14.
MATTER OF BRITTANY (1916)

        DRAW to the fire, and let us weave a web
           Of sounds and splendours intertwined –
              Of warriors riding two by two
              In silken surcoats stitched with blue,
[5]   To seek and strive the whole world through
           For a scarlet fruit with silver rind;
        Of unsteered ships that drift for miles on miles
        Amid the creeks of myriad magic isles
        Over enchanted seas, that leave at ebb
[10]   A beach of glittering gold behind.

        Hark! how the rain is rippling over the roofs
           And knocking hard on the window-pane!
              It rattles down the gutter-spout
              And beats the laurel-leaves about;
[15]   So let us tell of a kempy stout
           With bells upon his bridle-rein –
        How, as he rode beneath the chattering boughs,
        He clashed the iron visor over his brows,
        Hearing upon his heel the hurried hoofs
[20]   Of Breunor, Breuse or Agravaine.

        Of names like dusky jewels wedged in gold
           The tale shall cherish goodly store,
              Of Lionel and Lamorak
              And of Sir Lancelot du Lak,
[25]   And him that bore upon his back
           Arms for the Lady Lyonor;
        Persant, Perimones and Pertolepe,
        And Arthur laid in Avalon asleep,
        Dinas and Dinadan and Bors the bold,
[30]   And many a mighty warrior more.

And grimly crouched in every woodland way
   A dragon with his emerald eyes
      Shall sit and blink on passing knights;
      In the deep dells, old eremites,

[35]   Victors once of a thousand fights,
   Shall sing their masses at sunrise;
And weary men shall stumble unaware
On damsels dancing in a garden fair,
And there, like Meraugis of Portlesguez,

[40]   Dance, cheated of their memories.

To towns where we shall feast at Pentecost,
   Carlion or Kynke Kenadon,
      Each day shall come a faery dame,
      Or else a giant with eyes of flame

[45]   Shall bid to the beheading game
   Knights that the king sets store upon;
And some shall find, at hour of day's decline,
The house beside the fountain and the pine,
And learning much of marvel from their host,

[50]   Shall hasten greatly to begone.

Some, by the help of charmèd steeds shall – just –
   Leap through the whirling barriers
      That guard about the pleasant bower
      Where every moment is an hour,

[55]   And with an elfin paramour
   Drowse and dream for a hundred years,
But setting foot again on Middle Earth,
Or tasting wheaten bread in hour of dearth,
Shall crumble to a little cloud of dust

[60]   Blown by the wind across the furze.

Or sometimes through the arches of the wood
   The sad Good Friday bells will ring
      Loud in the ear of Percivale,
      Through many a year of ban and bale

[65]   Yet questing after the Sangraal
   For comfort of the Fisher King;

        And suddenly across a vault of stars
        Shall drive a network of enchanted spars,
        And Lancelot and Galahad the good
[70]   Behold the ship of hallowing.

        And first of all I'll tell the tale to you,
          And you shall tell the next to me:
            How gentle Enid made complaint
            While riding with her lord Geraint,
[75]   Or how the merry Irish Saint
          Went ever westward oversea;
        While your dim shadow moving on the wall
        Might be Sir Tristram's, as he harped in hall
        Before Iseult of Ireland, always true,
[80]   Or white Iseult of Brittany.

This poem was also included in the packet, entitled "Experiments in Metre," sent by Sayers to Miss Rowe in 1915. It was published first in *Fritillary*, Number 66 (December 1915), p. 42. It was then published in *OP. I* (1916), pp. 55-59. Besides modest punctuation variants, *OP. I* shows two minor word changes: *warrior* in line 15 becomes *kempy*, and *Kynkenadon* in line 42 becomes *Kynke Kenadon*.

15.
A MAN GREATLY GIFTED (1916)

        YOU are the song that a jester sang,
        Gambolling down the woods alone,
          When a wide, low, yellow moon
          Stared into the dusk of June;

[5]   And here and there, among the trees,
        Where sudden foxgloves showed like ghosts,
          The tiny streams, from edge to edge
          Slipped, smothered by the mossy ledge.

        The shadow dodged between the stems
[10]   Fantastically lengthening,
           And like a silly, sweet guitar,
           The little bells were all a-jar.

        O music swifter than a sword,
        Sharper than scent of spikenard,
[15]   Thus carelessly, to left and right
           Tossed by a jester in the night!

This poem appears in *OP.I*, p.60. It was reprinted in *Songs for Sale*, ed. E.B.C. Jones(Blackwell, 1918), p.38.

16.
THE ELDER KNIGHT (1916)

I

I HAVE met you foot to foot, I have fought you face to face,
I have held my own against you and lost no inch of place,
        And you shall never see
        How you have broken me.

[5]   You sheathed your sword in the dawn, and you smiled with careless eyes,
Saying "Merrily struck, my son, I think you may have your prize."
        Nor saw how each hard breath
        Was painfully snatched from death.

I held my head like a rock; I offered to joust again,
[10]   Though I shook, and my palsied hand could hardly cling to the rein;
        Did you curse my insolence
        And over-confidence?

You have ridden, lusty and fresh, to the morrow's tournament;
I am buffeted, beaten, sick at the heart and spent. –
[15]   Yet, as God my speed be
        I will fight you again if need be.

II

    A white cloud running under the moon
        And three stars over the poplar-trees,
    Night deepens into her lambent noon;
        God holds the world between His knees;
    Yesterday it was washed with the rain,
    But now it is clean and clear again.

    Your hands were strong to buffet me,
        But, when my plume was in the dust,
    Most kind for comfort verily;
        Success rides blown with restless lust;
    Herein is all the peace of heaven:
    To know we have failed and are forgiven.

    The brown, rain-scented garden beds
        Are waiting for the next year's roses;
    The poplars wag mysterious heads,
        For the pleasant secret each discloses
    To his neighbour, makes them nod, and nod –
    So safe is the world on the knees of God.

III

    I have the road before me; never again
        Will I be angry at the practised thrust
    That flicked my fingers from the lordly rein
        To scratch and scrabble among the rolling dust.

    I never will be angry – though your spear
        Bit through the pauldron, shattered the camail,
    Before I crossed a steed, through many a year
        Battle on battle taught you how to fail.

    Can you remember how the morning star
        Winked through the chapel window, when the day
    Called you from vigil to delights of war
        With such loud jollity, you could not pray?

Pray now, Lord Lancelot; your hands are hard
    With the rough hilts; great power is in your eyes,
Great confidence; you are not newly scarred,
    And conquer gravely now without surprise.

Pray now, my master; you have still the joy
    Of work done perfectly; remember not
The dizzying bliss that smote you when, a boy,
    You faced some better man, Lord Lancelot.

Pray now – and look not on my radiant face,
    Breaking victorious from the bloody grips –
Too young to speak in quiet prayer or praise
    For the strong laughter bubbling to my lips.

Angry? because I scarce know how to stand,
    Gasping and reeling against the gates of death,
While, with the shaft yet whole within your hand,
    You smile at me with undisordered breath?

Not I – not I that have the dawn and dew,
    Wind, and the golden shore, and silver foam –
I that here pass and bid good-bye to you –
    For I ride forward – you are going home.

Truly I am your debtor for this hour
    Of rough and tumble – debtor for some good tricks
Of tourney craft; – yet see how, flower on flower
    The hedgerows blossom! How the perfumes mix

Of field and forest! – I must hasten on –
    The clover scent blows like a flag unfurled:
When you are dead, or aged and alone,
    I shall be foremost knight in all the world –

My world, not yours, beneath the morning's gold,
    My hazardous world, where skies and seas are blue;
Here is my hand. Maybe, when I am old,
    I shall remember you, and pray for you.

This poem occupies pp. 61-65 of *OP. I*. Sections I and II were first printed under the title "To Strength" in *The Unique Manuscript Magazine*, September 1916, a publication privately compiled at the home of Dr. and Mrs. Dixey, friends of Dorothy Sayers's parents, and attributed to their children H. Giles and Maud; the original is possessed by the Bodleian Library, Oxford (MS. Eng. misc. e. 742, pp. 27-29). These same two sections also appear in the manuscript collection Sayers presented to Catherine Godfrey in 1915, only – inexplicably – they are offered as "*From the Mass in B minor*" where each is subtitled "To Strength." There are two minor changes in the text of the *OP. I* version; *sword* replaces *blade*, and *insolence* replaces *impertinence* in lines 5 and 11 of Section I. In line 40, *pauldron* and *camail* indicate *shoulder-armour* and *head-armour*, respectively. This poem was re-printed in *Songs for Sale*, ed. E. E. C. Jones Oxford: Blackwell, 1918), pp. 38-42; this I have not seen.

17.
HYMN IN CONTEMPLATION OF SUDDEN DEATH (1916)

LORD, if this night my journey end,
I thank Thee first for many a friend,
The sturdy and unquestioned piers
That run beneath my bridge of years.

[5] And next, for all the love I gave
To things and men this side the grave,
Wisely or not, since I can prove
There always is much good in love.

Next, for the power thou gavest me
[10] To view the whole world mirthfully,
For laughter, paraclete of pain,
Like April suns across the rain.

Also that, being not too wise
To do things foolish in men's eyes,
[15] I gained experience by this,
And saw life somewhat as it is.

<pre>
                    Next, for the joy of labour done
                    And burdens shouldered in the sun;
                    Nor less, for shame of labour lost,
[20]   And meekness born of a barren boast.

                    For every fair and useless thing
                    That bids men pause from labouring
                    To look and find the larkspur blue
                    And marigolds of a different hue;

[25]   For eyes to see and ears to hear,
                    For tongue to speak and thews to bear.
                    For hands to handle, feet to go.
                    For life, I give Thee thanks also.

                    For all things merry, quaint and strange,
[30]   For sound and silence, strength, and change,
                    And last, for death, which only gives
                    Value to every thing that lives;

                    For these, good Lord that madest me,
                    I praise Thy name; since, verily,
[35]   I of my joy have had no dearth,
                    Though this night were my last on earth.
</pre>

This poem was included in the manuscripts sent by Sayers to Miss Rowe in 1915 (and is now in the Bodleian Library, Oxford); it also appeared in *The Oxford Magazine*, 5 November 1915, p. 37. In *OP. I*, it appears on pp. 66-67. In both these publications, the stanza beginning "For eyes to see" has been shifted from an earlier position in the manuscript. Both publications also substitute *power* for *gift* in line 9. The records of David Higham Associates show permission granted to Thomas Crowell (Rinehart & Co.) to reprint this poem (11 December 1951), but there is no evidence of follow-up. The Marion E. Wade Center, Wheaton College, Wheaton, Illinois, has an autograph copy of this poem in "Poems: 1914-1915" (probably the original) (Wade/MS-167).

18.
EPITAPH FOR A YOUNG MUSICIAN (1916)

HERE was a man for whom time held the chance,
    If he had lived, of failure or success:
Failure of fame, which is a sore distress,
The world's applause, maybe, or tolerance.

[5] But God smote England in her dalliance,
    And like his fellows, neither more nor less,
        Here was a man.

So when death caught him in the haphazard dance,
    And robbed him of occasion to transgress,
[10]   He lost the chance of failure; perfectness
Was his alone. Stranger, rest here thy glance,
        Here was a man.

Published first in *The Oxford Magazine* (25 February 1916), this poem appears in *OP. I* on p. 68; there the subject is identified in a note at the bottom of the page by the first owner of my copy [K. I. R. Molyneux] as "E. A. A. F. / Corpus Christi." In the same hand, the date "June 1915" appears directly across the page from the identification. Barbara Reynolds (p. 52) completes the information: the young musician was Arthur Forest, a close friend of Sayers; he was killed in the Dardanelles. (See also *Letters of Dorothy L Sayers*, ed. Reynolds, vol I, pp. 89 - 91, 112.)

19.
TO M. J. (1916)

NOW that we have gone down – have all gone down,
    I would not hold too closely to the past,
    Till it become my staff, or even at last
My crutch, and I be made a helpless clown.

[5]   All men must walk alone, not drowse, nor drown
              Their wits, with spells of dead things overcast.
              Now that we have gone down, have all gone down,
          I would not hold too closely to the past.

          Therefore, God love thee, thou enchanted town,
[10]   God love thee, leave me, clutch me not so fast;
              Lest, clinging blindly we but grope aghast,
          Sweet friends, go hence and seek your own renown,
          Now that we have gone down – have all gone down.

This poem was first published in *OP. I* on page 70, but it was among the poems sent in manuscript by Sayers to Miss Rowe in 1915; it is now in the Bodleian Library, Oxford. This poem was one of the *rondeaux* especially mentioned to Miss Rowe, and it was accompanied by a parenthetical note: "(Ch. d' Orleans ABba ab AB abbaA)." Also in a note: "(5 beats)." The words *blindly clinging* (l. 11) have been reversed from the manuscript; *dearly* has been altered to read *closely* as above (l. 2); so also in line 8.

"M. J." was Muriel Jaeger, a contemporary of Sayers at Somerville, a fellow-author of the Going-Down Play, and the dedicatee of *Whose Body?*, where she is addressed "Dear Jim."

20.

LAST MORNING IN OXFORD (1916)

"The great poets ... are not at the pains of devising careful endings. Thus, Homer ends with lines that might as well be in the middle of a passage." –   *H. Belloc*

          I DO not think that very much was said
          Of solemn requiem for the good years dead.

          Like Homer, with no thunderous rhapsody,
          I closed the volume of my Odyssey.

[5]   The thing that I remember most of all
          Is the white hemlock by the garden wall.

June 23rd, 1915.

This poem, the last item in *OP. I* (p. 71) and the only one dated in the entire collection, underscores Sayers's affection for her Oxford days. The autograph copy of this poem in the Wade Collection at Wheaton College, Wheaton, Illinois, gives not only the date but also claims New College as the place of origin.

The cover of Sayers's second volume of poetry, 1918.

THESE CATHOLIC TALES WERE PRINTED AT THE VINCENT WORKS, OXFORD, AND FINISHED IN SEPTEMBER IN THE YEAR OF OUR LORD JESUS CHRIST, MDCCCCXVIII. PUBLISHED BY B. H. BLACKWELL, BROAD STREET, OXFORD, AND SOLD IN AMERICA BY LONGMANS, GREEN & CO., NEW YORK.

CATHOLIC TALES
BY DOROTHY L. SAYERS

OXFORD & B.H. BLACKWELL.

Three Shillings net.

Catholic Tales and Christian Songs, a collection of twenty-five poems, was the second book of Dorothy L. Sayers's poems published in Oxford by B. H. Blackwell. It appeared on 26 October 1918 in an edition of 1000 copies. (The cover bears only the short-title *Catholic Tales*.)

Barbara Reynolds notes (p. 81) that Sayers had offered the book previously to G. K. Chesterton, hoping that he would accept it for *The New Witness*: "The poems," she writes, "are much in his style and to a large extent inspired by his own robust and hearty expressions of faith." One poem, "Rex Doloris," was accepted and published earlier in the year in *The New Witness*.

21.
"ΠΑΝΤΑΣ ΕΛΚΥΣΩ" (1918)

Be ye therefore perfect.

You cannot argue with the choice of the soul.

Go, bitter Christ, grim Christ! haul if Thou wilt
Thy bloody cross to Thine own bleak Calvary!
When did I bid Thee suffer for my guilt
To bind intolerable claims on me?
[5]   I loathe Thy sacrifice; I am sick of Thee.

They say Thou reignest from the Cross. Thou dost,
And like a tyrant. Thou dost rule by tears,
Thou womanish Son of woman. Cease to thrust
Thy sordid tale of sorrows in my ears,
[10]   Jarring the music of my few, short years.

Silence! I say it is a sordid tale,
And Thou with glamour hast bewitched us all;
We straggle forth to gape upon a Graal,
Sink into stinking mire, are lost and fall . . .
[15]   The cup is wormwood and the drink is gall.

> I am battered and broken and weary and out of heart,
> I will not listen to talk of heroic things,
> But be content to play some simple part,
> Freed from preposterous, wild imaginings . . .
> [20] Men were not made to walk as priests and kings.
>
> Thou liest, Christ, Thou liest; take it hence,
> That mirror of strange glories; I am I;
> What wouldst Thou make of me? O cruel pretence,
> Drive me not mad so with the mockery
> [25] Of that most lovely, unattainable lie!
>
> I hear Thy trumpets in the breaking morn,
> I hear them restless in the resonant night,
> Or sounding down the long winds over the corn
> Before Thee riding in the world's despite,
> [30] Insolent with adventure, laughter-light.
>
> They blow aloud between love's lips and mine,
> Sing to my feasting in the minstrel's stead,
> Ring from the cup where I would pour the wine,
> Rouse the uneasy echoes about my bed . . .
> [35] They will blow through my grave when I am dead.
>
> O King, O Captain, wasted, wan with scourging,
> Strong beyond speech and wonderful with woe,
> Whither, relentless, wilt Thou still be urging
> Thy maimed and halt that have not strength to go? . . .
> [40] Peace, peace, I follow. Why must we love Thee so?

This poem's title is a phrase from the Greek text of St. John's Gospel, xii.32: ἐξω; κἀγω εαυ υψωθω εκ τηδ γηδ Παυτας ἐλκυσω Προδ εμαυτον

"And I, if I be lifted up from the earth, *will draw all* men unto me." The mood is reminiscent of much of George Herbert and also of Francis Thompson's "Hound of Heaven." The first epigraph is drawn from St. Matthew v. 48. I suspect that the second epigraph derives from St. Augustine, whose *Cibus sum grandium* was on

Sayers's mind about this time. (See her *Strong Meat*, p. 9.) This poem appears on pages 12-13 of *Catholic Tales and Christian Songs*.

In 1946, she was informed by a young music instructor at Williams College in western Massachusetts that he had a short while previously set the opening lines of this poem to music for a men's chorus, not knowing the author or the origin of the lines. In the meantime he was able to track down the name of the author and to learn the title of the poem. She used the occasion to chide him gently for failing first to secure permission and to pay a fee before any public performance. (The correspondence is possessed by the Marion E. Wade Center, Wheaton College, Wheaton, Illinois.)

22.
DEAD PAN (1918)

At the hour of Christ's agony a cry of "Great Pan
is dead!" swept across the waves in the hearing of
certain mariners; and the oracles ceased. PLUTARCH.

For we know that the whole creation groaneth and
travaileth together in pain until now.

I fill up on my part that which is lacking of the
afflictions of Christ.

AND there was darkness over all the land
Three hours; and in the dark so wild a cry
That all men hearing sought to understand
What thing it was that in such pain must die.

[5] But there was darkness, so that none may say
What there befel, except the midnight bird
Whose staring face is still struck white to-day
For blank amaze at all he saw and heard.

He that maintained unblinded vigil there
[10] Told us: "There were vast shapes which loomed and grew
Around, and He was fearfully changed: I swear
They were goat's feet the nails had stricken through.

"How mourned pale Isis, 'neath the hideous rood
Crouched in the dust! How passed in one fierce sound
[15] Side-smitten Balder! For what grim festal food
Smoked forth the blood of Mithra to the ground?

"But Pasht my cousin, the wise African,
Looked from the judgment hall toward the North,
And knew all things fulfilled when thus began
[20] The deathless Ritual of the Coming Forth;

"For One came treading those eternal floors
That was the Word of the tremendous Book,
Crying throughout the long-drawn corridors
So that the porters of the pylons shook:

[25] "I am Osiris! and the gates reeled back
Before the God twin-crowned with white and red,
And an echo rose and went in the wind's track
Over the Middle Sea: Great Pan is dead! . . .
Whereat the oracles fell mute," he said.

The epigraph attributed to Plutarch is drawn from his *Isis and Osiris* and sustained by one of the essays in his *Moralia*, "de defectu Oraculorum." The other two epigraphs are citations respectively from The Epistle of St. Paul to the Romans (viii. 22) and The Epistle to the Colossians (i. 24). The poem appears on pages 28 and 29 of *Catholic Tales and Christian Songs*. Thematically, Sayers's poem parallels Milton's "On the Morning of Christ's Nativity," where Christ is identified with "the mighty Pan," and cessation of the oracles follows His birth; in Sayers's poem, the focus of action, however, is on the death of Christ/Pan. All nature ("the whole creation groaneth and travaileth together in pain") felt the blow, as did gods of various mythologies.

Interestingly enough, Sayers returns to this subject in the Eleventh Play of *The Man Born to be King* ("King of Sorrows") when Claudia, the wife of Pilate, reports her dream at the time of Christ's crucifixion:

I was in a ship at sea, voyaging among the islands of the Aegean. At first the weather seemed calm and sunny – but presently, the sky darkened – and the sea began to toss with the wind . . . Then, out of the east, there came a cry, strange and piercing. . . .

> (*Voice, in a thin wail*
> "Pan ho megas tethnéke –
> Pan ho megas tethnéke –")

and I said to the captain, "What do they cry?" And he answered, "Great Pan is dead." And I asked him, "How can God die?" And he answered, "Don't you remember? They crucified him. He suffered under Pontius Pilate" . . . .

Not only the death of Christ but also his leading captivity captive from hell are handled in a somewhat Blakean manner. (For what it is worth, one should note that Sayers undoubtedly also knew Elizabeth Barrett Browning's *The Dead Pan*.)

In l. 6, *midnight bird* = a white-faced owl; l. 9, *He that maintained unblinded vigil* = the anonymous reporter who identified Pan with Christ; l. 12, *goat's feet* = allusion to Pan; l. 13, *Isis* = in Egyptian mythology the sister and wife of Osiris; l. 15, *Balder* = the central figure of Norse tree mythology; l. 16, *Mithra* = the representative of Persian mythology; l. 17, *Pasht* = African (non-Egyptian) myth figure; l. 20, *Ritual of the Coming Forth* = a reference to fertility rites, pre-figuring the Resurrection; l. 24, *pylons* = gateways of an Egyptian temple; l. 25, *Osiris* = Egyptian god of the dead, murdered by the god Set but resurrected.

23.
REX DOLORIS (1918)

Signed with the sign of His Cross and salted with
His salt. S. AUGUSTINE

"WHEREFORE wilt thou linger, Lady Persephone?
The sheaves are gathered, the vintage is done,
Bacchus through the ivy leaves laughing with his satyrs
Calls us to the feasting, and the ripe, red sun
[5] Drops like an apple, tumbling to the westward,
The shout of the Maenads is merry on the hill,
Why do the wheat-ears fall from thy fingers?
Whom dost thou look for, lingering still?

"Whom does thou look for? Here is one to woo thee,
[10] Brown-cheeked, beautiful, lissom as the larch,
Lightsome, slender, blossomy with kisses,
Merrier-footed than the winds in March;
Loose thy hair to dream along his shoulder,
Drowse in thy whiteness warm upon his breast,
[15] He shall feed thee with wheaten cakes and honey
And all fair fruits that are rich and daintiest."

"I weary of the feast, I weary of the harvesting,
I weary of your music, children of the earth –
Your feet dance over the roofs of my palaces,
[20] The halls of Hades ring hollow to your mirth;
The great King of Grief hath reft me, ravished me,
Broken me with kisses, conquered me with pain,
I have drunk his bitter wine, I have eaten of His pomegranates,
Can find no savour in the honeycomb again."

[25] "Wherefore wilt thou linger, Lady Persephone,
When sheaves are gathered and the vintage is done,
And Bacchus through the ivy leaves laughing with his satyrs

>   Calls to the feasting, and the ripe, red sun
>   Drops like an apple, tumbling to the westward,
> [30]   While the shout of the Maenads echoes from the hill?"
>   "Ere the round moon rise ruddy on the corn-shocks
>   The Lord of Hades shall have me at His will."

This poem, which appears on pages 30 and 31 of *Catholic Tales and Christian Songs*, was first published in G. K. Chesterton's *The New Witness*, 26 April 1918, page 591; the punctuation and capitalization are more precise than in *Catholic Tales* (pp. 30-31). "The great King of Grief," "The Lord of Hades" who will have the Lady Persephone "at His will," has by his act so affected the world of Nature, among other things, that the old patterns – e.g., the rape of Proserpine – are forever divinely altered by the redemption. This is the ideal meaning of the epigraph from St. Augustine.

24.
SACRAMENT AGAINST ECCLESIASTS (1918)

>   BETWEEN the Low Mass and the High,
>   Between the Altar and my cell,
>   I met Christ and passed Him by,
>   And now I go in fear of Hell.
>
> [5]   My dying brother Ninian
>   Confessed himself to me and said:
>   "I find the Christ in every man,
>   But how comes He in wine and bread?"
>
>   I cursed my brother as he died,
> [10]   "Absolvo" I would not repeat,
>   I bare away the Crucified,
>   I would not sign his breast and feet.
>
>   I lifted Christ above my head,
>   I kneeled to Him, I bare Him up,
> [15]   And Christ cried to me from the bread,
>   Christ cried upon me from the cup:

> "What is this bitter sin of thine,
> So little to have understood, . . .
> To find Me in the bread and wine
> [20] And find Me not in flesh and blood?
>
> "Go, say thy Mass for Ninian,
> That, when he comes to Heaven, maybe
> His prayer shall save thee, righteous man . . .
> If he can find the Christ in thee!"

This poem appears on page 32 of *Catholic Tales and Christian Songs*. It shows what unChristlike attitudes and behaviour may obtain when Christianity becomes so institutionalized – so hardened in abstract liturgical form ("in the letter") – that it is blinded to true implications ("the spirit").

25.
BYZANTINE (1918)

Jesus Christ, the same yesterday and to-day and for ever.

> I SIT within My Father's house, the Lord God crucified,
> My feet upon the altar-stone set straitly side by side,
> My knees are mighty to uphold, My hands outstretched to bless,
> My eyelids are immutable to judge unrighteousness.
>
> [5] What though the bitter winds of war lay waste the house of prayer?
> They cannot shake My quiet robe nor stir My folded hair,
> I wrestled in Gethsemane, I cried and I was slain,
> Never, for any strife of men, to strive nor cry again.

> I sit within My Father's house, with changeless face to see
[10] The shames and sins that turned away My Father's face from Me;
> Be not amazed for all these things, I bore them long ago
> That am from everlasting God, and was and shall be so.

This poem, which appears on page 35 of *Catholic Tales*, is an ironic presentation of a view of a Christ who cannot "be touched with the feeling of our infirmities," in contradistinction to the Epistle to the Hebrews (iv. 15-16) from which the epigraph is taken (xiii. 8). It is by inference a rejection of the vaunted imperturbability of a Byzantine Christ, artistically identifiable but spiritually unacceptable. Especially is this poem pertinent to the period which witnessed in World War I "the bitter winds of war" that "lay waste the house of prayer." The poem is virtually a condemnation of a Christology whose passion is all in the past.

26.
PYGMALION (1918)

> THEREFORE one day, as all flesh must, she died,
> Just as the mowers brought the last load in
> From happy meadows warm with summer-tide,
> And through the open casement, far and thin,
[5] The nightingale's first music did begin.

> "Love is the sum of this world's whole delight,
> Love," said the bird, "the ending of desire,
> Love brought us, timid, forth to the lovely light,
> Love the sole outlet, love, both toil and hire,
[10] Love, with whose death the songs of life expire."

> Yet, as the limbs turned stone and bitter-cold,
> Widowed Pygmalion sat beside the bed,
> Huddling dry-eyed to see the new grown old
> Again so strangely, and his clamorous head
[15] Jarred him with discourse; and at length he said:

"Marble, my white girl, marble! Cyprian thighs
And amorous bosom all made chaste once more,
As though no lips had ever kissed thine eyes
To slumber – virgin as they were, before
The feet of Venus glowed along the floor! . . .

"Thy beauty should have made the workman blind
That found thee buried in the dust of thrones
Hereafter, when our pomps are left behind
Like some strange, sprawling scale of barbarous tones,
Our temples turned to curious heaps of stones;

"When by the highways merchant folk shall go
Three feet of earth above our walls and towers,
And other than Grecian ships bear to and fro
New wares, new men, and all as brief as flowers –
Thou hadst outlasted all that time devours.

"But thou art dead; thou art flesh and art dead;
The grave will be thy lover, thy round breast
Nourish the worm, while, shred by ghastly shred,
The mouth that laughed, the fingers that caressed,
Wither, O dearest of my works and best! . . .

"What have I gained? some mornings when my soul
Leaped out of me into the arms of day,
When the world, like a chariot, span in my own control,
Times when I saw the beech-tree leaves a-sway
And knew how green they were and far from grey.

"Say I learned joy – this was indeed a gain;
But can I face the reckoning unafraid?
For joy I bartered, first, that ancient pain
Which stabbed me into vision; next, betrayed
All that men looked for in me; thus I paid.

"Yea, I that rated at a small amount
That strange, cold jewel, purchased unawares,
Men's gratitude – I that no longer count
For anything in any man's affairs,
Am doubtful now; thus the gods grant our prayers.

>   "Ay me undone! The world cries out to me:
>   'Pygmalion the sculptor, where art thou?' –
>   Buried indeed, O buried hopelessly
>   Fathom-deep under, fathom-deep under now –
> [55] The curious rootlets pry about his brow . . .
>
>   "There is no remedy; what is changed is changed;
>   No skill can rub out wrinkles from the heart,
>   Nor even God knit friends that are estranged
>   As innocently again as at the start,
> [60] Since they must keep the memory of that smart
>
>   "For good or evil still. So I return
>   Never to that old quiet which asked no beat
>   Of answering pulse, content alone to burn,
>   While no fierce hand might fret thy bosom sweet,
> [65] Nor any lover come betwixt thy feet.
>
>   "I wrought thee for the world, and then thou wast
>   Immortal – and I wept uncomforted;
>   But since I made thee mine – O thou art lost
>   To me and all men. I was glad," he said,
> [70] "But thou art dead, O thou art dead, art dead."

This poem was first published in *Oxford Poetry 1918*, pp. 46-48. Sayers was herself one of the editors of the volume which was published by Blackwell. The poem is signed "Dorothy L. Sayers (Somerville)."

27.
THREE EPIGRAMS (1919)

I

[-----'s new watch, for which I don't think she gave enough, loses large po r t i o n s o f time at irregular intervals].

>   PONDER the Scriptures closely in thy youth,
> [5] And thou mayst glean good store of worldly truth;
>   "Even in riches let thy trust be small,"
>   – And in cheap goods put thou no trust at all.

II

[After two hours' practical entomology in the cabbage-patch].

[10] POET! think not the jealous gods contrive it
         That you have still the toughest chop to chew,
      Nor, officer, conceive the simple Private
         A happier man than you,

      Nay, in this world compact of grub and grabbage
[15]   (My sensitive young friend) experience shows
      The worm lies curled heart-deep within the cabbage
         As in the cabbage rose.

III

[That the service of the Superman is harder than the service of Heaven].

[20] "COWARDS", the ancient proverb saith,
      "Die many times before their death":
      Yet, when the bombs come bursting round
      Most of us are cowards found.
      Now "dying daily"'s decent, – it
[25] Has been enjoined by Holy Writ,
      But dying nightly, when it grows habitual! –
      O Superman! I do not like your ritual.

This poem, first found on pages 103-104 of the *Unique Manuscript Magazine*, XII (1919), is identified solely by the initials "D. S." beneath the title. The handwriting is not Sayers's; it appears to be that of H. G. Dixey, who edited the material (Bodleian MS. Eng. misc. e. 743). Cited by permission of the Bodleian Library, Oxford.

In l. 7, *"Even in riches let thy trust be small"* = apparently a paraphrase of either Proverbs xi.28 or I Timothy vi.17; l. 9, *entomology* = study of insects; l. 15, *grabbage* = a coinage for *garbage*; l. 19, *Superman* = unlikely that this is a reference to G. B. Shaw's drama; more likely a reference to Nietzsche's *Übermensch*, what the strutting aggressor likes to consider himself; l. 21, *"Cowards die many times"* = used by Shakespeare in *Julius Caesar*, II,ii,32, and also by Michael

Drayton in *Mortimeriados*, l. 2723; l. 23, *bombs* = allusion to warfare bombardment; l. 24 "*dying daily*" = see I Corinthians xv.31.

28.
FOR PHAON
WITH "THAT ETERNITIE PROMISED BY OUR EVER-LIVING POET." (1919/1920)

> WHY do you come to the poet, to the heart of iron and fire,
> Seeking soft raiment and the small things of desire,
> Looking for light kisses from lips bowed to sing?
> Less than myself I give not, and am I a little thing?
> [5] I walk in scarlet and sendal through the dry plains of hell,
> And fine gold and rubies are all I have to sell,
> For I am the royal goldsmith whose goods are all of gold,
> And you shall live for ever like a little tale that is told;
> When kings pass and perish and the dust covers their name,
> And the high, impregnable cities are only wind and flame,
> The insolent new nations shall rise and read, and know
> What a little, little lord you were, because I loved you so.

This poem was first published by Blackwell in February 1920 in *Oxford Poetry 1919* on page 50; the next two poems ("Sympathy" and "Vials Full of Odours") appeared on the next pages of the same publication. They were acknowledged as the work of "D. L. SAYERS / SOMERVILLE)." Sayers herself was one of the editors of the volume, the other two being T. W. Earp and Sacheverell Sitwell. Some of the other contributors to the volume were Vera M. Brittain, J. B. S. Haldane, V. de S. Pinto, and D. A. E. Wallace.

Phaon was the legendary boatman of Mitylene favoured by Aphrodite with youth and beauty because he had ferried her across the sea without charge; legend also says that because he rejected Sappho she destroyed herself. But the point of the poem is that because Phaon sought Sappho for less than genuine love, he would forever be remembered as "little" – her love for him, unreturned, would cause her forever to be remembered as great in love.

The sub-title is taken from Thomas Thorpe's "Dedication" of Shakespeare's collected sonnets published in 1609.

29.
SYMPATHY (1919/1920)

    I SAT and talked with you
    In the shifting fire and gloom,
    Making you answer due
    In delicate speech and smooth –
[5]   Nor did I fail to note
    The black curve of your head
    And the golden skin of your throat
    On the cushion's golden-red.
    But all the while, behind,
[10]   In the workshop of my mind,
    The weird weaver of doom
    Was walking to and fro,
    Drawing thread upon thread
    With resolute fingers slow
[15]   Of the things you did not say
    And thought I did not know,
    Of the things you said to-day
    And had said long ago,
    To weave on a wondrous loom,
[20]   In dim colours enough,
    A curious, stubborn stuff –
    The web that we call truth.

This poem was first published in *Oxford Poetry 1919* on page 51.

30.
VIALS FULL OF ODOURS (1919)

    THE hawthorn brave upon the green
    She hath a drooping smell and sad,
    But God put scent into the bean
    To drive each lass unto her lad.

[5]   And woe betide the weary hour,
For my love is in Normandy,
And oh! the scent of the bean-flower
Is like a burning fire in me.

Fair fall the lusty thorn,
[10]   She hath no curses at my hand,
But would the man were never born
That sowed the bean along his land!

This poem was published in *Oxford Poetry 1919* on page 52. It was published earlier in *The Oxford Chronicle*, No. 4370, 30 May 1919, page 13, column b. It was reprinted as "The Bean Flower," with a musical setting by E. J. Moeran, and published in London in 1924 by J. & W. Chester, Ltd. Moeran, as Christopher Dean informs me, was a member of the Oxford and Cambridge Musical Club, which met in Bloomsbury in the early 1920s.

31.
OBSEQUIES FOR MUSIC (1921)

Baritone Solo	"DEAD Past, go forth, bury thy carrion dead
	Because they do offend me grievously."
Recit.	Full sternly thus I said,
	And my dead Past obediently
[5]	Rose up to bury its dead.
Strings	And first went my dead loves, all fair and frail
	And very, very pale,
	And through their tinsel garments the chill wind
	Blew; and the grey rain slantingly
[10]	Swept in long streaks across their faces thinned.
	Some of them had been strangled, one struck dead;
	But most of them had died for lack of bread.
Solo flute	And with fantastic steps at the procession's head
	Went a tall piper, piping delicately: –
Choir [15]	"Carry us out, carry us out, carry us out and lay us by –

	Far away from the noise of things take and bury us quietly,
Woodwind	Let the grass grow over us,
	And the still earth cover us.
	Remember no more, remember no more, remember no more how once we were;
[20]	Starved souls, unworthy souls – this was a burden we could not bear,
	There is nothing on earth so cold
	As dead love turned to mould.

"Laugh for pity, laugh for pity, laugh for pity – do not weep,
Sour green fruit of a half-grown tree, know we never were made to keep;
[25] Ere we were ripe we fell,
And truly it is well."

Organ Agnus Dei, Agnus Dei,
Dona eis requiem.

Solo With sound of solemn trump majestical
[30] Next the procession of my dead hopes came;
Tuba and Strings Long, white and stiff they lay, whose heads had once topped heaven,
Crowned each with tapering flame;
Stiff, long and white beneath the golden pall
Which no wind stirred, so heavily it hung;
[35] Their bright wings were not riven,
But folded gently up they sheltered death
Tenderly, splendidly in a jewelled sheath;
But over every heart the narrow wound and deep
Of a sharp knife driven
[40] Showed where the blood had drained away in sleep.

And as they went, on this wise it was sung: –

Choir "We that were great are very pitiful,
We that are dead were very beautiful –
Full There was no soul in us,
Orchestra [45] This is the goal for us,
Let the bell toll for us.

"We that had wings could never leave the earth,
We that went robed in gold were little worth –
Make no more tarrying
[50] Since you are carrying
Us to our burying.

"Fancy on vanity begat us all,
No strength had we, although so fair and tall –
One prick of pain in us,
[55] Our life was slain in us,
God's peace remain with us."

Organ Agnus Dei, Agnus Dei,
Dona eis requiem.

Harp Then went a heavenly music harping high,
[60] And in that sound, behold! dead grief was carried by.

Solo Sorrows I saw, like wizened, wan old men,
Strings Small, with shrunk limbs; I saw their long, lean hands
Whose clutch in that far time had been like iron bands,
But now was impotent, because since then
[65] Ever from day to day,
As the veins failed and sinews fell away,
The grip slacked from my throat,
And I could thrust grief far from me and note
What was the message of his pallid eyes.

Harp [70] So my dead griefs went by me side by side,
And it was of old age that all of them had died.

And thus one sang to sound of psalteries: –

Choir "Your guests we were, we sat beside your board,
And all you could afford
Full [75] You gave to us – we ate and drank and stayed:
Orchestra You grew afraid.
Some came from off the sea and some from land,
A dark and pirate band,
But some of us you did yourself call in –
[80] Yours was the sin.

	"Only one gift we ask of you to-day:
	To carry us away;
	Keep no memorial of us; we are gone;
	Let us alone.
[85]	"Do not embalm the body of cold care;
	You have received your share –
	The price we paid for food and tenement
	Is changed and spent."
Organ	Agnus Dei, Agnus Dei,
[90]	Dona eis requiem.
Solo	Dead hatreds too – I saw their bodies pass
	Solemnly borne, and covered, that no eye
	Might mark their hideous features. Yet alas!
Horns and	Through the thin pall
Trombones [95]	Each swollen, ghastly form I dimly might descry
	And in my fantasy remould them all,
	From head to foot uncouth,
	Squat, horrible of shape,
	Each like an ape
[100]	Mowing with sideways and distorted mouth.
	And these had rotted ere they came to die,
	And through the livid air a noisome dew did fall.
Three Horns	This was the singing that before them went,
	Croaked to a rusty instrument: –
Choir [105]	"Bury us quickly, ere bone fall from bone,
	And eager sunshine rot us into life,
Brass and	And the swarms
Wood-wind	Of white worms,
	Seeking, hiding,
[110]	Swiftly gliding
	Through a mesh
	Of riddled flesh,
	Wound in coils of playful strife,
	Reap the crop that you have sown.

[115]	"Bury us quickly, ere we haunt your sleep
	With our puffed blackness and our bolting eyes,
	And the smell
	Unbearable
	Of decaying;
[120]	All delaying
	And all pride
	Set aside.
	Shame the sexton swiftly plies
	His tool, and digs our trenches deep."
Organ [125]	Agnus Dei, Agnus Dei,
	Miserere, Domine.
Solo	Then in an endless file they bore my follies spent,
	And this time verily for shame I bent
Solo Bassoon	And would not look upon them as they went,
[130]	Till in my ear a voice chirped mockingly:
	"One of us is immortal still with thee."
Guitar	In treble all a-jar
	This was sung falsely to a cracked guitar: –
Choir	"No tablets of enduring brass be seen,
[135]	No threnodies be heard,
Strings pizz.	Our memory is green, young soul, is green
Soli Oboe and	And endlessly absurd.
Bassoon	Whatever passes in the grave away,
	Your hair, your lips, your eyes,
[140]	Remembrance in the Resurrection Day,
	And we with it, shall rise.
	"How silly was your yesterday, young friend,
	To-day is sillier still –
	Will you grow silliest as you near the end?
[145]	O yes, be sure you will."
Organ	Agnus Dei, Agnus Dei,
	Dona eis requiem.

Solo	Then dropped the music mute and stumblingly
	A pauper burial, stark and black and grim,
Timpani and [150]	Plashed in the roadway dim;
Muted Strings	Tatters of mist hung on the sordid hedge,
	Each sorry pall was taken out of pledge,
	Each coffin was bestowed on me
	By workhouse charity;
[155]	And here, poor wretches, dressed in borrowed rags,
	Unwept, unloved, contemptuously borne out,
	Went poor, dead unbelief and poor dead doubt.
	Their wet, wan faces, worn with war and rout,
	Their bodies twisted with fatigue and fear,
[160]	Hunger that drives and drags,
	And drenching cold, that knots up heart and limb;
	Yea, it was plain to see
	All had died slowly, struggling, dreadfully; –
	This was the dismal hymn we had to hear: –
Choir [165]	"We toil and sweat, and strive, and die,
	And find no bed in which to lie.
Five Horns	"Each dreadful night, each hopeless morn,
	We wear what other men have worn.
	"We toil to cross an empty plain,
[170]	We eat the wind and drink the rain.
	"We grow more ugly day by day –
	For God's sake put us all away."
Organ	Agnus Dei, Agnus Dei,
	Dona eis requiem.
Clarinet [175]	These therefore came with shows and sound
Choir	Unto a hallowed space of ground,
Full Orchestra	Wherein a young and radiant priest
	Stood. On his shoulder was a spade,
Tuba	And there with shining hands he made
[180]	A garden, looking toward the east.

The title of this poem (signed "DOROTHY L. SAYERS"), published in *London Mercury*, III (January 1921), pages 249-253, is curious. The way musical accompaniment is stressed (although, of course, there is no musical notation) might lead one to expect a lament for music, whereas the title must mean "obsequies which may be set to music."

There *is* a funeral procession, punctuated by a liturgical refrain, which invites the reader to accept the passing-away of "dead loves" (lines 6-26), of "dead hopes" (lines 30-56), of "dead griefs" (lines 60-88), of "dead hatreds" (lines 91-124), of "follies" – not all yet deceased (lines 127-145), and of "poor, dead unbelief and poor dead doubt" (lines 148-172). The Latin liturgical refrain, "Agnus Dei, Agnus Dei, / Dona eis requiem," is chivalrously answered in the final strophe of the poem.

While the entire poem may seem to some readers a bit factitious, there are many apt phrases suggesting psychological acuity – the only quality a confession may convincingly bear. The lines are skilfully modulated, the irregular line-lengths and rhyme-schemes resulting in an odic form. The music imagery supports the psychological thrust. The year 1921, incidentally, saw major works in verse by Robert Graves, Victoria Sackville-West, and Edith Sitwell; it was the year before T. S. Eliot's *The Waste Land*.

In a letter to her mother (22 January 1921), Sayers delivered a conviction based upon her mother's reaction to this poem: "what I have always maintained – you can never judge of a poet's life by his words!" She amplified this statement: "The most cynical passages of that gloomy work were written at the beginning of my second year at College," carrying the implication that her poetry did not reflect the mood of her personal life at the time. But one may object that she doth protest too much. (See *Letters*, ed. Reynolds, Vol I, p.174.)

J. C. Squire (1884-1959) was the Editor of *London Mercury* from 1919 to 1931. His own *Collected Poems*, published posthumously in 1959, had an introduction by John Betjeman.

32.
THE POEM (1921)

Kiss me! It cannot be that I
    Who wove such songs of pain and fire
Last night – that fierce, desiring cry –
    It cannot be that I should tire?

[5] Prove to me, prove you're not grown weak,
    Break down this citadel of sense,
Show me myself too faint to speak,
    Not armoured in my eloquence.

I swear my singing was begun
[10]   Out of love's black and bitter deep –
But oh! the work was so well done
    I smiled, well-pleased, and fell on sleep.

Now all day long I must rehearse
    Each passionate and perfect line,
[15] Mine the immaculate great verse –
    I do not know the thoughts for mine.

This poem, which develops the strange divorce between imaginative self-fulfilment and physical actuality, was first published in *London Mercury*, IV (October 1921), 577. It was reprinted in *The Mercury Book of Verse* (London: Macmillan, 1931), page 227, and also in J. C. Squire, ed. *Younger Poets of Today* (London: Martin Secker, 1932), page 431, the version printed above. (Some of the other poets anthologized in this 1932 volume include Richard Aldington, Owen Barfield, Edmund Blunden, Roy Campbell, George Rostrevor Hamilton, Richard Hughes, Aldous Huxley, C. Day Lewis, V. Sackville-West, Siegfried Sassoon and Edith Sitwell.).

Barbara Reynolds points out that this is the period of Sayers's liaison with John Cournos (pp. 107-116).

33.
ON GUINNESS (1935)

> If he can say as you can
> Guinness is good for you
> How grand to be a Toucan
> Just think what Toucan do.

Appears in Brabazon (p. 135). Sayers and John Gilroy (later Sir John) worked together on advertising campaigns for Colman's and for Guinness during her time at S. H. Benson. Brabazon writes: "Many people still remember Dorothy's original jingle that accompanied Gilroy's picture of the Toucan, his great bill poised over two glasses of Guinness."

In August 1981, Sir John Gilroy wrote:

> The Guinness toucan seems to be just as famous now as he was nearly fifty years ago. Of course, he wasn't a toucan to begin with. I originally drew him as a pelican with 7 pints of Guinness balanced on his beak. Underneath, I wrote the following verse:
>
>> A wonderful bird is a pelican,
>> Its mouth can hold more than its belly can.
>> It can hold in its beak
>> Enough for a week;
>> I simply don't know how the hellycan!
>
> Dorothy L. Sayers [who had been] a copywriter...at the S. H. Benson advertising agency was brought in to make my pelican acceptable and tone it down. The poem she wrote transformed my pelican into a toucan. And that's how the toucan was born.

(From a printed label attached to a reproduction of the advertisement, signed by Gilroy, in the possession of Barbara Reynolds.)

34.
"HERE LIES THE BODY OF SAMUEL SNELL" (1934)

      Here lies the Body of SAMUEL SNELL
      That for fifty Years pulled the Tenor Bell.
      Through Changes of this Mortal Race
      He Laid his Blows and Kept his Place
[5]   Till Death that Changes all did Come
      To Hunt him Down and Call him Home.
      His Wheel is broke his Rope is Slackt
      His Clapper Mute his Metal Crackt,
      Yet when the great Call summons him from Ground
[10] He shall be Raised up Tuneable and Sound.

            MDCXCVIII
            Aged 76 years

This pleasant poem is found in *The Nine Tailors* (1934), III, The First Part, "The Quick Work". Hezekiah Lavender, the aged bell-ringer, is exulting in his certain prospect of excelling the longevity of a predecessor who had pulled Tailor Paul in ringing the changes of the bells in Fenchurch St. Paul for fifty years. He is cleaning the inscription on the tomb of his competitor, and he volunteers the opinion that "they don't write no sech beautiful poetry these here times." See Barbara Reynolds, ed. *The Letters of Dorothy L. Sayers* (London: Hodder and Stoughton, 1995), Vol. I, pp. 364-365.

One must admire Sayers's talent for constructing this example of a period-piece. For Samuel Snell, who died in 1698, she provided a sustained and apt "metaphysical conceit," full of puns attached to change-ringing, to form this inscription, which surely would have rejoiced the heart of the John Milton who wrote the Hobson poems.

35.
FROM *GAUDY NIGHT* (1935)

>Here, then, at home, by no more storms distrest,
>   Folding laborious hands we sit, wings furled;
>   Here in close perfume lies the rose-leaf curled,
>Here the sun stands and knows not east nor west,
>Here no tide runs; we have come, last and best,
>   From the wide zone through dizzying circles hurled,
>   To that still centre where the spinning world
>Sleeps on its axis, to the heart of rest.
>
>Lay on thy whips, O Love, that we upright,
>   Poised on the perilous point, in no lax bed
>   May sleep, as tension at the verberant core
>Of music sleeps; for, if thou spare to smite,
>   Staggering, we stoop, stooping, fall dumb and dead,
>   And, dying, so, sleep our sweet sleep no more.

[5] appears beside line 5; [10] appears beside line 10.

This sonnet appears in Sayers's *Gaudy Night*, the tandem work of Harriet Vane and Peter Wimsey; she composed the octave, he, the sestet. This was a fitting structural gesture in the novel in the light of its theme.

Harriet Vane has much to say about her inspiration and procedure in composing the octave. Conducive factors include the time of the year, the aura of place, the quietude which she calls a "melodious silence," the refreshing recall of her "singing voice, stifled long ago by the pressure of the struggle for existence, and throttled into dumbness by that queer, unhappy contact with physical passion" [the Philip Boyes affair, narrated in *Strong Poison*]. This was the matrix of a burst of poetic expression. "Great golden phrases, rising from nothing and leading to nothing swam up out of her dreaming mind…" "A detached pentameter, echoing out of nowhere, was beating in her ears" …; "it had the feel of a sonnet;" "she fumbled over rhyme and metre, like an unpractised musician fingering the keys of a disused instrument;" "the metre halted monotonously, lacking a free stress-shift, and the chime 'dizzying-spinning' was unsatisfactory;" "The lines swayed and lurched in her clumsy hands, uncontrollable;" "still, such as it was, she had an octave;" "She could find no turn for the sestet to take, no epigram, no change of mood;" "In the meanwhile she had got her mood on paper – and this is the release that all writers, even the feeblest, seek for as men seek for love...." She shut her notebook.

Some days later she discovered that Peter, to whom she had loaned the note-book containing a dossier of the Shrewsbury College scandals, had completed the sonnet! She first berates herself for leaving the half-finished sonnet "mixed up [in her note-book] with one's detective work for other people to see!" Lord Peter's only comment written on the composition ("A very conceited, metaphysical conclusion") educed from Harriet Vane various emotional remarks laced with admiration for his skill, and then a final sharp judgment: "It was not one of the world's greatest sestets, but it was considerably better than her own octave: which was monstrous of it." (*Gaudy Night*, Chapters XI and XVIII)

See my article "From Poetaster to Poet: An Aspect of the Character Development of Lord Peter Wimsey," *Seven* [the Sayers Centenary issue], 1993.

36.
AUPRÈS DE MA BELLE (1937)

All in my father's garden
The lilacs blow so high,
And all the birds of heaven
Will rest there by and by.
[5] *In my lady's bosom*
Sweet it is to lie.

The blackbird & the throstle,
The laverock in the sky,
And my sweet amorous turtle
[10] Whose song is all a sigh.

>   She sings of luckless ladies
>   For lack of love who die;
>   For me my turtle sings not,
>   A lovely lad have I.
>
> [15]   Where lies your lover, lady [,]
>   These many days gone by?
>   Within a German prison
>   My lovely lad doth lie.
>
>   What would you give, my lady,
> [20]   To have your lover nigh?
>   I'd burn the Tower of London
>   And let the Thames run dry.
>
>   I'd give the Bank of England,
>   St. Paul's & Peckham Rye,
> [25]   And my sweet amorous turtle
>   To have my lover nigh.

The Wade Center, Wheaton College, Wheaton, Illinois, possesses the autograph of this adaptation by Sayers of "Auprès de ma Blonde," [or, Belle] the French folk-song used in the play *Busman's Honeymoon*. The French original, on the other hand, was used in the novel, which appeared later than the play. I am grateful to Robert A. Scott, Collection Assistant of the Wade Center, for pointing out to me this adaptation. Lord Peter sings lines from the adaptation in the beginning of Act II, and in Act III he is joined by Harriet in singing additional lines. Still later, Lord Peter sings more. This autograph adaptation is cited by permission.

L. 8, *laverock* = variant of lark; ll. 9, 13, 25, *turtle* = now archaic for *turtledove*; l. 17, *German prison* = an adaption of "Hollande" in the original; ll, 21-24, *Tower of London, Thames, Bank of England, St. Paul's, Peckham Rye* = all London sites offered by the lady to have her lover nigh, corresponding to "Versailles, Paris et St, Denis" in the original.

37.
THE ZODIACK (1937)

To the Lady Zenocrate
her most fortunate
Starres
wisheth Prosperitie
R. W.

March – Aries

    The Sunne like Jason from exile returning
    Triumphant nowe putts on hys fleece of golde
    And wth his iolie heat doth set on burninge
    Alle that of late was watrie dull and coolde.
[5]   On budding boughe the cuchat softe complayneth
    Vnder the thorne the Harte doth seek the Hinde
    No solitarie thynge on Earth remayneth
    Saue onlie mee that proue thee still vnkinde.
    For shame bee not to Loue soe late a comer
[10]   To fade and falle thy fruitinge still vndone,
    Or thinkst thou ther shal be noe end to Sumer?
    Consider how short increase hath the Sunne.
    But vi brief monethes behold his lusty shining
    Ere to the Scorpions Nest he goes declining.

April – Taurus

    See the poore bayted bulle on euerie side
    By dogges hemmed in, this waie and that he wheeles,
    One nips his tender muzzle, one his side
    Doth teare, another frets him at the heeles.
[5]   With lowered hed he snuffs, he stamps the ground,
    He flings them backe yet still they come anon
    Makying him madde wth many a grieslie wounde
    While idle men stand by to loo them on.
    Wherein the ymage of fond loue thow viewest
[10]   Whom thy sharp scornes do dogge with angrie spight
    Thou daie and nighte the vnequal course renewest

>   Clapping thy handes to see him bleed and fight
>   Whose piteous state thy too hard harte upbraids
>   That bloudie showes should giue delight to mayds.

May – Gemini

>   Sitt downe by mee that I maie reade thy face
>   As pale divines pore on a holy booke,
>   If ther be anie text of hope or grace
>   In that smooth parchment that so faire doth looke.
> [5]   Alas tis like Sibyllaes pages writ
>   A redeles riddle to my wit opposing,
>   Or if my hart interpret for my wit
>   I feare my gloss shall proue no more than glozing.
>   For louers art is but a false assayer
> [10]   Finding that goolde it did before conceal,
>   Thus I from silence wring assent to prayer
>   And make thy lookes the glasse to mine owne zeal.
>   Lo in thy pregnant eyes twin babes do moue,
>   And I of both the patterne, Pitie and Loue.

June – Cancer

>   The crooked crabbe, close armed cap-a-pe
>   Like cunning caitiff sly doth sidewaies goe
>   And from his castle gate in braue arraie
>   Brandysshe his pinching armes to fright the foe.
> [5]   Poor seelie foole, his cunning helps him nott,
>   Nor walls of rock to him proue nothing worth,
>   For he by greede is ta'en in wicker Pott,
>   That hath a smooth road in but no road forth.
>   So I was arm'd, so I didde turne and winde
> [10]   So I by sence was snar'd in dedly gin;
>   Loue was the bait, and being caged I finde
>   No waie to leape the poyntes that fence me in.
>   I climb, I falle; I toyle yet gaine no inch.
>   Soe, being in, 'tis I must beare the pinch.

July – Leo

        Lo nowe the Lyon in his burning sign
        Shakes his broad mane to fyre the Galaxy
        And on his backe the Sunne Prince Palatine
        To his bright Palace bears, that all the skye
[5[Shows like a furnace of clere molten golde
        Whence heauenlie heat and heauenlie radiance streames,
        And highest Alps throw off their nightcaps colde
        Feeling the warmth of those celestiall beames.
        Loue that to this dull globe art light and sunne
[10]   A lyon in myght and as the lyon fiers
        Putt furthe thy power whiles yett it may be done
        Ne tarie til old Time thy strength disperse,
        Ere Winters raine shall quench hott Julies fyre
        O burne, burne, burne, inflaming her desire.

August – Virgo

        Howe long wilt thou putt on mee this disdaine? –
        Pluck out my beard and whip me back to schoole
        To spell the criss-cross row ouer againe,
        For nowe I seem a childe, a boye, a foole,
[5]   And but an emptie boast mine age appeareth;
        Indeed, faire Loue, thou dost mee too much wronge
        That while the ripening yeere to haruest weareth
        Keep barren winter thus a twelvemoneth longe.
        In his sixth house the strong Sunne takes his pleasure,
[10]   Wth kindlie fruits the Earth's wide wombe doth breede
        Whose sweet iuice burst and overruns the measure
        The golden eare plump wth the swelling seede.
        Can Phebus' heat burne in the Virgin's brest
        Yet I, that am more hott, still finde thee chaste?

September – Libra

        Nowe haue I seen beneath the sable valance
        Of Heauens high canopy the glittering Scales
        Hold night and daye fixt in an equal balance,
        That for a little space neither preuailes.

[5]   Now Phoebus with hys feet astride the line
       Tuggs at the beame, yet all too light light proues
       To counteruaile the leaden darkes decline,
       Slow through her quadrant downe the long night moues.
       Griefe is but heauiness and grieuous paine,
[10] And all delight is light as vanity,
       Why seeke I than to reckon loss or gaine?
       That which can dout the Sun can outdo mee.
       Yet hang my scales leuel for one short breath,
       Here light, loue, life; there night, and hate, and death.

October – Scorpio

       Like as a Tree in a greene garden set
       By careful gardeners hand norysshed and tended
       Whose infant shootes wth crystall showres are wet
       And from sharp winds and scorching heats defended,
[5]   While a short time no inward wounde it feeleth
       Florysseth forthe and shows both floure and seede,
       Then sodein droops and being plucked up revealeth
       The secret Worme that on hys roote doth feede;
       I that was yong and braue in lustihood
[10] Bearing the blossoms of my hopeful Spring
       Am nowe become a drie and dying wood
       Whereon the dusty leaues hang withering;
       My Summer past, my Autumn hath no fruit,
       The Scorpions sting hath perced to my hart roote.

November – Sagittarius

       Still must I turne uppon Ixxions wheele
       That scars maie bide the turninge of the yeere?
       Or beare the pryckes of thy blinde Archers steele
       Whom a more deadlier darte doth thret soe neere?
[5]   For lo the Sagittarie veild in clowde
       Stands wth his arwe drawne upp to the hed,
       What skills it than to be soe cruel proude
       To him that soon shal noe more torments dred?
       Noe noe lett bee, it growes too late for playing,

[10]   Dull nyghte brings on the rayne and winds blow chill,
    And lustie youth that ons rode forth on maying
    Now wth sad stepps goes creepying downe the hill.
    Euen Maiedaie sports end wth the falling darke –
    Wilt thou shoot on till Deth remoue the marke?

December – Capricornus
    Sovthwarde ye Sunne ys gone, would I might followe
    Where Pan forth tripping on light goatish feete
    Leadeth the Satyr crewe with song and hollo
    Foreuer pyping to his Syrinx swete.
[5]   Sovthwarde ye Sunne ys gone, on euerie hande
    Within hys pleasaunte courtes meridionall
    The Cypress talle and fruitfull Oliue stande
    And thro the ayre softe balmie Dewes doun falle.
    Southwarde hees gone; but yett as Caesars maie
[10]   From cittie high thir vtmost boundes controule
    Hee setts a windowe open daie by daie
    A lyttel space vnto ye Northern pole
    Ruling farre off from these distressfull jarres
    Our wynter and our melancholic Starres.

Januarie – Aquarius
    Flow downe you riuers you salt riuers flowe
    You sad salt riuers to the center downe
    Downe downe flowe downe you mournfull waters slowe
    To where deep Lethe wth obliuioun
[5]   Washes the feet of ouer trauaild manne.
    Run not apace but softlie softlie falle
    Teares that too swift haue run time and agen,
    For nowe are run out tears and time and all.
    Tears are our water clock to mete out time
[10]   Our moments sand within times turning glasse
    Our mirth a brazen jacke that strikes the chime
    Our life the gnomons shadowe that doth passe
    Dayly to marke ye passing of the lyghte
    Itselfe the ymage and the hew of nyghte.

POETRY OF DOROTHY L. SAYERS

Letter to Mistres Muriel Byrne Penned by Dorothy L. Sayers

Februarie – Pisces

        Farewel proud harte the Sunne wth sullen face
        Dips through the Ocean to the siluerie Fysshe
        Quenching his fiers beames in that watrie place.
        Nothinge is nowe to hope nothinge to wishe.
[5]   Noe light noe heat no health no ioie no loue
        No sence noe sighte noe ear noe breath noe harte;
        No fear noe griefe noe anguysshe more can moue
        Mee that from sunne light life and heat must parte.
        Come come repent nott nowe ti all in vaine
[10]   Noe spell can call back Phaethon from his sleepe
        Nor euer kindle the quick fyres againe
        In this sad harte that drowned lies doe deepe.
        Alle things that moue in the coolde brinie fludde
        Are coolde – so Deths sharp sea makes chill my bludde.

The collection of poems, of which "The Zodiack" is the longest, was composed by Sayers and presented to Muriel St. Clare Byrne on 18 April 1937 with a covering letter, all copied out in Elizabethan script, purportedly the work of Roger Wimsey in 1585. All the poems in this group are love poems which possess the flavour and tone of sixteenth-century English amorous poetry. "The Zodiack" is a remarkable fabrication of the English sonnet-sequence vogue of the last two decades of the century, featuring the spurned lover who remains faithful whatever discouragements or vicissitudes arise. Sayers has very cleverly assembled examples of the irregularities of orthography, verb forms, mechanics, and punctuation of the period. "The Zodiack" is, to be sure, not strictly astrological; it follows conventional seasonal changes.

Sayers presented these poems to Miss Byrne in acknowledgement of the latter's help in writing the play *Busman's Honeymoon*. But why did she go to the trouble of simulating Elizabethan documents? Quite simply, she sought to compliment her friend (also a former Somerville College student) in partial recognition of Miss Byrne's scholarly achievements – especially her work on the Lisle manuscripts (which she was to continue for many additional years) and her distinctive work on deciphering Elizabethan handwriting.

Professor R. B. McKerrow in his *An Introduction to Bibliography for Literary Students* (Oxford: Clarendon Press, 1928) writes of Miss Byrne's work in an area which was preparatory to her decipherment of the Lisle letters – her "Elizabethan Handwriting for Beginners": "I know of no elementary introduction to the subject except that in Miss M. St. Clare Byrne's very useful article [*The Review of English Studies*, i. 198 ff., 1925].... to which I am indebted for several points in the pages which follow" (p. 341,n.). It was no child's play for Sayers to prepare these simulated documents, and it is important to note that the quality of the poems demonstrates convincingly that the extended interval of detective-fiction writing had not quelled her impulse to produce competent poetry, however much the work may resemble a tour-de-force.

The version here was deciphered by the late C. W. Scott-Giles, OBE, FSA, Fitzalan Pursuivant of Arms Extraordinary, in December 1976. (Mr. Scott-Giles also gave attention to Lord Roger Wimsey's poetry in *The Wimsey Family: A Fragmentary History Compiled from Correspondence with Dorothy L. Sayers* (London: Gollancz, 1977).

It remains to be said that I have presented "The Zodiack" beginning with the March entry because it seemed to me that this was Sayers's intention by having Lord Roger sign off after the February entry, thus following the order of months as it was observed in sixteenth-century England.

It will be remembered that Miss Byrne was to be co-editor with Sayers of the only-partially-completed Bridgeheads series which began with Sayers's *The Mind of the Maker*. See Reynolds, page 313.

See also my article "For Miss Byrne" in the *Festschrift* presented to Dr. Barbara Reynolds on her eightieth birthday, 13 June 1994.

The original materials, including the letter to Miss Byrne, are in the Wade Collection at Wheaton College, Wheaton, Illinois, and are here reproduced by permission.

38.
TO THE INTERPRETER HARCOURT WILLIAMS (1939)

"What I have done is yours; what I have to do is yours; being part in all I have, devoted yours."

Sound without ear is but an airy stirring,
Light without eyes, but an obscure vibration,
Souls' conference, solitude, and no conferring,
Till it by senses find interpretation;
[5] Gold is not wealth but by the gift and taking,
Speech without mind is only passing vapour;
So is the play, save by the actor's making,
No play, but dull, deaf, senseless ink and paper.

Either for either made; light, eye; sense, spirit;
[10] Ear, sound; gift, gold; play, actor; speech and knowing,
Become themselves by what themselves inherit
From their sole heirs, receiving and bestowing;
Thus, then, do thou, taking what thou dost give,
Live in these lines, by whom alone they live.

This magnificent sonnet, one of the best poems Sayers ever wrote, was printed among the prefatory pages of *The Devil to Pay*, the second Canterbury Festival play she produced (1939), as a dedication to the actor who had created both William of Sens and Faustus.

In her will, Sayers left to Williams and Frank Napier (also involved in both *The Zeal of Thy House* and *The Devil to Pay*) the copyrights and the playing rights of *The Zeal of Thy House*, little knowing that both men would predecease her. She drew up her will on her birthday, 13 June 1939. Williams's death occurred on 12 December 1957, just five days before Sayers's own.

To corroborate the sincerity of Sayers's conviction about the importance of the actor, one should note what she wrote later in *The Mind of the Maker*: "To hear an intelligent and sympathetic actor infusing one's own lines with his creative individuality is one of the most profound satisfactions that any imaginative writer can enjoy; more – there is an intimately moving delight in watching the actor's mind at work to deal rightly with a difficult interpretation, for there is in all this a joy of communication and an exchange of power." (Methuen p.52.)

As Barbara Reynolds notes (p. 280), the quotation preceding the sonnet is from Shakespeare's dedication of *The Rape of Lucrece* to the Earl of Southampton.

39.
THE ENGLISH WAR (1940)

"What other race on earth, well aware of its danger, isolated to fight, would utter a great sigh of relief that all had abandoned it, and say to itself: 'Well, thank goodness for that; now we know where we are'?"

PHILIP JORDAN, in a broadcast.

PRAISE God, now, for an English war –
    The grey tide and the sullen coast,
The menace of the urgent hour,
The single island, like a tower,
[5]   Ringed with an angry host.

This is the war that England knows,
    When all the world holds but one man –
King Philip of the galleons,
Louis, whose light outshone the sun's,
[10]   The conquering Corsican;

When Europe, like a prison door,
    Clangs; and the swift, enfranchised sea
Runs narrower than a village brook;
And men who love us not, yet look
[15]   To us for liberty;

When no allies are left, no help
    To count upon from alien hands,
No waverers remain to woo,
No more advice to listen to,
[20]   And only England stands.

This is the war we always knew,
    When every county keeps her own,
When Kent stands sentry in the lane,
And Fenland guards her dyke and drain,
    Cornwall, her cliffs of stone;

When from the Cinque Ports and the Wight,
    From Plymouth Sound and Bristol Town,
There comes a noise that breaks our sleep,
Of the deep calling to the deep
    Where the ships go up and down,

And near and far across the world
    Hold open wide the water-gates,
And all the tall adventurers come
Homeward to England, and Drake's drum
    Is beaten through the Straits.

This is the war that we have known
    And fought in every hundred years,
Our sword, upon the last, steep path,
Forged by the hammer of our wrath
    On the anvil of our fears.

Send us, O God, the will and power
    To do as we have done before;
The men that ride the sea and air
Are the same men their fathers were
    To fight the English war.

And send, O God, an English peace –
    Some sense, some decency, perhaps
Some justice, too, if we are able,
With no sly jackals round our table,
    Cringing for blood-stained scraps;

No dangerous dreams of wishful men
    Whose homes are safe, who never feel
The flying death that swoops and stuns,
The kisses of the curtseying guns
    Slavering their streets with steel;

> No dreams, Lord God, but vigilance,
>   That we may keep, by might and main,
> Inviolate seas, inviolate skies; –
> But, if another tyrant rise,
>   Then we shall fight again.

[60]

This stirring patriotic poem by Sayers appeared in *The Times Literary Supplement*, 7 September 1940 (Volume 2014), page 445, slightly more than a year after England declared war on Germany in World War II. The poem was prominently printed in italics within a border of double rules and carried the name of the poet in capital letters at the end.

The poem was reprinted in *The Best Poems of 1941*, selected by Thomas Moult (London: Jonathan Cape, 1942), on pages 38-40; other poets included among the seventy-six in the collection were Laurie Lee, C. Day Lewis, Stephen Spender, and Lawrence Whistler. The poem also appeared in *The Terrible Rain: The War Poets 1939-1945*, edited by Brian Gardner (London: Methuen & Co., 1966), on pages 45-47; some of the other poets included in this anthology were W. H. Auden, C. Day Lewis, Anne Ridler, Edith Sitwell, and Stephen Spender. The poem also appeared in an earlier collection, *Other Men's Flowers* (London: Jonathan Cape, 1948), which I have not seen.

Captain A. R. Williams informed Sayers after the war that when he was private secretary to Lord Wavell as Viceroy of India (1943-1947) he heard the Viceroy recite from memory the entire poem "The English War."

40.
"LORD, I THANK THEE –" (1942)

       IF IT were not for the war,
       This war
       Would suit me down to the ground.
       There are things about it which pander to my worst
           instincts,
[5]   Flatter my weak points,
       And make me a prig and a Pharisee.

       I have always detested travelling,
       And now there is no travelling to do.
       I need not feel that I ought to be improving my mind
[10]   By a visit to Rome, the Pyramids, the Pyrenees,
       New York or New Guinea,
       Or even Moscow;
       I have never really panted to contemplate Fuji-Yama,
       And now I need not bother about it;
[15]   I need not feel abashed by people who take their holidays
           on the Matterhorn
       Or navigating the Fiords;
       I can sit quietly in Essex and feel superior
       When my friends complain
       That they cannot get on without a sea-voyage or sea-bathing,
[20]   (I abominate cold water),
       That they feel stifled
       Without a breath of mountain air.

       I was born in a hollow
       At a confluence of rivers,
       I was brought up in a swamp
       Carved, caged, counter-checked like a chessboard
       By dyke and drain,
       Running from the Great Ouse to the Wash,
       Where the wind never stops blowing;
[30]   I know all about the smell that comes off the drowned land
       When the waters turn home in the spring

(A peculiar smell – and I have encountered something like it
In Venice
In the *piccoli canali* in the moonlight,
[35] Where it is considered highly romantic);
I can say to the gadabouts:
"If you must have dank smells, you can get them in the Fens of East Anglia;
If you must break your necks on a precipice
You can do it with perfect discomfort
[40] In Cumberland;
And there are apple blossoms in Kent,

Blue seas on the Cornish coast,
Conifers in Scotland;
But I shall stay at home,
[45] Indulging my natural laziness,
And save petrol and coal for my country;
And if anybody requests me
To deliver unnecessary speeches in remote parts of the country,
I can plead the difficulties of war-time travel,
[50] And suffer no pangs of conscience.

I detest bananas,
A smug fruit, designed to be eaten in railway carriages
On Bank Holidays,
With a complexion like yellow wax
[55] And a texture like new putty
Flavoured with nail polish.
Yes, we have no bananas,
Glory be!
And the hygienic people
[60] Who eat prunes and grape-fruit for breakfast
Are cast into outer darkness
Gnashing their dentures.
Why should anybody eat breakfast
For its edifying qualities,
[65] Or its slimming properties,
Or its improving influence

Upon the skin and the bowels?
Behold, the moral has put on immortality,
And the last shall be first
[70] In the economy of managed consumption.
I do not take sugar
In tea or coffee (even black coffee);
I can give it away to my neighbours,
Purchasing their grateful affection
[75] At no cost to myself –
If everybody was made like me
The Ministry of Food would rejoice.
I need not buy new clothes,
Or change for dinner,
Or bother to make up my face –
It is virtuous to refrain from these things,
I need not shiver in silk stockings; –
I had a hunch about wool before it was rationed;
Now I have knitted myself woollen stockings
[85] That come a long way up.
They are warm and admirable,
They do not ladder or go into holes suddenly.
I can boast quietly about them
And smirk while others admire my industry;
[90] As it happens, I like knitting
And nothing gratifies one more
Than to be admired for doing what one likes.
In London there are still shops
With silk stockings in the windows
[95] ("Positively the last release");
I see the women and the girls
Check in their stride, stop, gaze in hungrily,
Fumbling with handbags, calculating coupons,
Yielding to temptation.
[100] Poor souls!
They will never be able to walk through the rose-garden
Or play with the kitten
But anxiety will gnaw at their hearts like a demon rat;

> The crack of a snapping stitch
> Will sound in their ears like the crack of doom.
> But I shall walk cheerfully in woollen
> This winter, and the next, and the next,
> Hand-knitted without coupons;
> And the old lisle stockings will do for the summer –
> If there is any summer.
>
> It is jolly to take up a newspaper
> And find it so thin!
> The ruthless restriction of twaddle
> Is a rare, refreshing fruit
> Better than many bananas.
> The Woman's Page,
> The Sports Page,
> The Feature Page,
> The Page of Bathing Beauties,
> Are clipped as close as Samson's skull,
> Together with the Comic Strip
> And the God-wottery Corner for Garden-lovers.
> The blare of the advertisements,
> Imploring, cajoling, stimulating, menacing, terrifying
> An apathetic public
> Into buying what it neither needs nor desires,
> Has dwindled into an apologetic murmur.
> Regretting the shortage of supplies,
> Whispering pathetically, "Forget-me-not,
> Forget me not when good times come again!"
> We are not electrified every other day
> By the bursting into the world,
> With accompaniments suitable to the advent of a long-promised Messiah
> Of a new soap.
> Soap is rationed.
> (I always thought we washed far too much anyhow –
> Animals do not wear out their skins
> And destroy their natural oils

THE POEMS 127

	With perpetual washing;
[140]	Even the cat despises soap,
	And who ever heard of a cow washing behind the ear?)
	There is very little room these days
	For the misreporting of my public utterances;
	Soon they will not be reported at all,
[145]	Thank goodness!
	And, curiously enough, books and plays seem to do better
	When nobody reviews them.
	Also, owing to the lack of paper
	The demand for books exceeds the supply –
[150]	A thing that has not been known
	Since they started all this popular education and cheap printing.
	Nobody ever wants a thing
	Until it is taken away –
	We used to have far too much of everything.
[155]	I can now enjoy a more glorious victory,
	More exultation of spirit,
	By capturing a twopenny tin of mustard
	Or a packet of hairpins
	And bearing it home in triumph
[160]	Than I could have achieved before the war
	By securing a First Folio of Shakespeare
	At vast trouble and expense
	In the sale-room [.]
	The local chimney sweep
[165]	Keeps hens.
	He takes the scraps from my table, the kitchen scraps,
	And the hens return them to me,
	By a beautiful economy of nature,
	In the likeness of eggs.
[170]	A new-laid egg
	Will bind a friendship
	Faster than it binds a cake;
	A string of onions

                    Is a gift more gracious
[175]   Than a necklace of pearls;
                    I am better off with vegetables
                    At the bottom of my garden
                    Than with all the fairies of the *Midsummer Night's Dream.*
                    If it were not for the war,
[180]   This war
                    Would suit me down to the ground.

This amusing poem by Sayers was her contribution to a work edited by her friend Storm Jameson, *London Calling* (New York and London: Harper & Brothers, 1942), pages 293-298. Other contributors included Rebecca West, Walter de la Mare, Noel Streatfield, J. B. Priestley, Harold J. Laski, Osbert Sitwell, John Masefield, Sheila Kaye-Smith, E. M. Forster, Edmund Blunden, Bonamy Dobrée, Frank Swinnerton, Phyllis Bottom, Helen Waddell, E. M. Delafield, Phyllis Bentley, H. E. Bates, Robert Graves, Lettice Cooper, Mary Agnes Hamilton, G. M. Trevelyan, T. S. Eliot, Angela Thirkell, Captain Liddell Hart, C. Day Lewis, Kate O'Brien, Rose Macaulay, and, of course, Storm Jameson herself. Quite a galactic assemblage!

This poem was also printed in *Britain*, I (November 1942), on pages 37-41; and, in a limited edition of one hundred copies, the Sayers poem was printed by itself at the Overbrook Press in Stamford, Connecticut, in January 1943.

Composed in free verse, this poem is conversational in style. It alludes to Sayers's birth in Oxford, her upbringing in Bluntisham in the Fen country, her being sought as a celebrity speaker, her long-standing quarrel with those guilty of inaccuracy of reporting in the press. Atmosphere of war-time is indicated exclusively by reference to non-belligerent concomitants.

Line 26, *counter-checked* = restrained (See Sayers's "The Fen Floods: Fiction and Fact," *The Spectator*, No. 5675 [2 April 1937], pages 611-612.); l. 34, *piccoli canali* = (Italian) little canals; l. 53, *Bank Holidays* = days on which English banks are legally closed, usually observed as general holidays; l. 120, *clipped as close as Samson's skull* = allusion to the story in Judges xiii-xvi; l. 122, *God-wottery* = affected or over-elaborate, especially of gardens, from *If God wot* in T. E. Brown's poem (1876) on gardens; l. 161, *First Folio of Shakespeare* =

the first collection of Shakespeare's plays, published in 1623, a treasured rarity.

41.
FROM *THE MAN BORN TO BE KING* (1943)

THE MAKERS

  The Architect stood forth and said:
    "I am the master of the art:
  I have a thought within my head,
    I have a dream within my heart.

[5]   "Come now, good craftsman, ply your trade
    With tool and stone obediently;
  Behold the plan that I have made –
    I am the master; serve you me."

  The Craftsman answered: "Sir, I will;
[10]   Yet look to it that this your draft
  Be of a sort to serve my skill –
    You are not master of the craft.

  "It is by me the towers grow tall,
    I lay the course, I shape and hew;
[15]   You make a little inky scrawl,
    And that is all that you can do.

  "Account me, then, the master man,
    Laying my rigid rule upon
  The plan, and that which serves the plan –
[20]   The uncomplaining stone."

  The Stone made answer: "Masters mine,
    Know this: that I can bless or damn
  The thing that both of you design
    By being but the thing I am;

[25] "For I am granite and not gold,
  For I am marble and not clay,
You may not hammer me nor mould –
  I am the master of the way.

"Yet once that mastery bestowed
[30]   Then I will suffer patiently
The cleaving steel, the crushing load,
  That makes a calvary of me;

"And you may carve me with your hand
  To arch and buttress, roof and wall,
[35] Until the dream rise up and stand –
  Serve but the stone, the stone serves all.

"Let each do well what each knows best,
  Nothing refuse and nothing shirk,
Since none is master of the rest,
[40]   But all are servants of the work –

"The work no master may subject
  Save He to whom the whole is known,
Being Himself the Architect
  The Craftsman and the Corner-stone.

[45] "Then, when the greatest and the least
  Have finished all their labouring
And sit together at the feast,
  You shall behold a wonder thing:

"The Maker of the men that make
[50]   Will stoop between the cherubim,
The towel and the basin take,
  And serve the servants who serve Him."

The Architect and the Craftsman both
  Agreed, the Stone had spoken well;
[55] Bound them to service by an oath
  And each to his own labour fell.

This poem appears on pages 7 and 8 of *The Man Born to be King*. It follows a dedication to Val Gielgud and precedes the Foreword by J. W. Welch. I must thank Christopher Dean for pointing out that lines 37-52 were selected by the Girl Guides Association and published, with acknowledgement to Sayers, in *Notices for Commissioners* (London, 1947), p. 135. The subject of good work was very prominent in the thinking and writing of Dorothy L. Sayers during the last two decades of her life. In the Introduction to these very plays, Miss Sayers writes "a work of art that is not good and true *in art* is not good and true in any other respect. . . ." (p. 20).

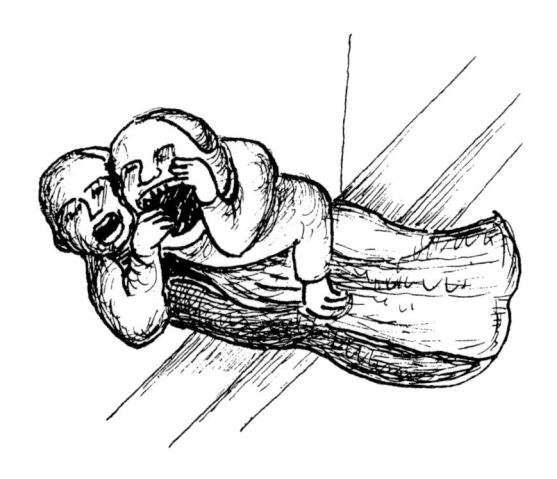

42.
AERIAL RECONNAISSANCE (1943)

YES – it's marvellous how they take these photographs –
marvellous –
what does the explanation say?
The white splotches are blast
[5] and the black blobs are craters,
and the little speckly bits
are sunlight shining through windows upon the floor inside,
showing that the roof's off –
yes, quite –
[10] The power-house has been hit,
it doesn't look much of a hole,
but doubtless the bomb exploded and damaged something
important
that one can't see;
those things like shadowy safety-pins
[15] are ships sunk in the harbour –
this one is down by the bows
and this by the stern
and that –
(marked H, dear, see what it says) –
[20] Oh! that one's still afloat; well,
I suppose it's all right
but it looks just the same as the others –
yes, of course, *they know*,
but you really have to be an expert
[25] to interpret these things,
naturally they don't mean anything much to the layman,
but of course I am quite convinced
that the destruction was enormous –
absolutely convinced –
[30] absolutely.

What? the papers have come?
Thank you, thanks;
Now I suppose they will tell us –

Oh, look!
[35] look!
but *I know* this picture –
that's real,
something that means something
that I can interpret for myself
[40] without any arrows and diagrams,
something that I have seen,
and known from a child,
standing on the Seven Holes Bridge at Earith
looking across the washes
[45] to the Isle of Ely
over the drowned fen stretched out sullen and silent
in the last redness of a level sun.
Nine exclamation marks standing in a row –
those are poplars,
[50] (the same old poplars)
desolate at the road's verge
with their feet in the water
and the wind melancholy in their sighing height;
and there, the thin black ribbon,
[55] the crest of the dyke,
nibbled at the edge, you see –
if you keep your eye on it
there will come a little heave in the grey-silver,
and the line will just shorten quietly,
[60] become fragmentary,
break up into dots,
settle down like a sleeper
drawing the blanket smoothly over a hunched shoulder.
There is the causeway
[65] tipping suddenly into oblivion
from off the chequer-work of the patched fields;
and there – delicate parallels
drawn with a snapping-pen on white paper –
the railroad,
[70] the permanent way,

over which trains must go very softly,
feeling forward,
throwing up a bow-wave like a ship –
softly, you see, because
nobody can tell what is happening
to the embankment
hidden, helpless, under the hungry water
that licks it away, greedy and secretive,
like the tongue of a great cat –
(they will be wiser to hold up all the traffic
or there might be a nasty accident).
Here, where road and rail cross,
there must have been a bridge of some sort....
Where has it gone? – I can tell you –
I know where it is –
Here, where I put my finger,
five miles down-river, at the bridge below,
baulks and beams and loose stones battering against the piers,
piling under the blocked arch in the swollen eddy and gurge –
I never saw that at home (though it has happened)
but I have seen the ice come down the Great Ouse
packed and swirling, a-jostle, choking the water-gates,
putting the river in a rage....
                                        What is all *that*?
Oh, that?
that is a village, of course,
water-logged over the eaves by the look of it,
twenty foot deep, that means,
or possibly thirty...
no, no – it will drain off in a few days,
leaving a curious and characteristic smell,
and mud,
extraordinarily fine and clinging, you'd be surprised....
No, I shouldn't think it would do much good
to the insides of dynamos
and machines and things....
The land? that's different,

| | it won't hurt the land
| | unless, of course, the place is swampy by nature
| | and the condition becomes permanent,
| [110] | in which case
| | they will have the job of reclaiming it all over again –
| | but injury to the land
| | was not, one supposes, a primary objective. . . .

| | Well, I must say,
| [115] | those are wonderful pictures,
| | I am delighted to have seen them –
| | let me have the paper when you have finished with it,
| | I want to look again,
| | and go on looking
| [120] | because I recognize this,
| | because I know what it means, and understand it,
| | because I can see exactly what we have done –
| | we have blown up the dams,
| | burst the sluices,
| [125] | unshackled the waters.

This poem appeared in *Fortnightly*, New Series 154, No. 922 (October 1943), pages 268-270.

One should, of course, re-read Sayers's *The Nine Tailors* for narrative replication, or "The Fen Floods: Fiction and Fact," *The Spectator*, No. 5675 (2 April 1937), 611-612.

Line 88, *baulks* = timbers; l. 89, *gurge* – (dialectal) whirlpool.

43.
WAR CAT (1943)

I AM SORRY, my little cat, I am sorry —
If I had it, you should have it;
but there is a war on.

No, there are no table-scraps;
[5]   There was only an omelette
Made from dehydrated eggs,
and baked apples to follow,
and we finished it all.
The butcher has no lights,
[10]   The fishmonger has no cod's heads —
There is nothing for you
but cat-biscuit
and those remnants of yesterday's ham;
You must do your best with it.

THE POEMS

[15] Round and pathetic eyes,
baby mouth opened in a reproachful cry,
how can I explain to you?
I know, I know –
"Mistress, it is not nice;
[20] the ham is very salt
and the cat-biscuit very dull,
I sniffed at it, and the smell was not enticing.
Do you not love me any more?
Mistress, I do my best for the war-effort;
[25] I killed four mice last week,
Yesterday I caught a young stoat,
you stroked and praised me,
you called me a clever cat.
What have I done to offend you?
[30] I am industrious, I earn my keep;
I am not like the parrot, who sits there
using bad language and devouring
parrot-seed at eight-and-sixpence a pound
without working for it.
[35] If you will not pay me my wages
there is no justice;
if you have ceased to love me
there is no charity.

See now, I rub myself against your legs
[40] to express my devotion,
which is not altered by any unkindness.
My little heart is contracted
because your goodwill is withdrawn from me;
my ribs are rubbing together
[45] for lack of food,
but indeed I cannot eat this –
my soul revolts at the sight of it.
I have tried, believe me,
but it was like ashes in my mouth.
[50] If your favour is departed
And your bowels of compassion are shut up,

           then all that is left me
           is to sit in a draught on the stone floor and look miserable
           till I die of starvation
[55]   and a broken heart."

           Cat with the innocent face
           What can I say?
           Everything is very hard on everybody.
           If you were a little Greek cat,
[60]   or a little Polish cat,
           there would be nothing for you at all,
           not even cat-food:
           indeed you would be lucky
           if you were not eaten yourself.
[65]   Think if you were a little Russian cat
           prowling among the cinders of a deserted city!
           Consider that pains and labour,
           and the valour of merchant-seamen and fishermen
           have gone even to the making of this biscuit
[70]   which smells so unappetizing.
           Alas! there is no language
           in which I can tell you these things.

           Well, well!
           if you will not be comforted
[75]   we will put the contents of your saucer
           into the chicken-bowl – there!
           all gone! nasty old cat-food –
           The hens, I dare say,
           will be grateful for it.

[80]   Wait only a little
           and I will go to the butcher
           and see if by any chance
           he can produce some fragments of the insides of something.
           Only stop crying
[85]   and staring in that unbearable manner –
           as soon as I have put on my hat
           we will try to do something about it.

My hat is on,
I have put on my shoes,
[90] I have taken my shopping-basket –
What are you doing on the table?

The chicken-bowl is licked clean;
There is nothing left in it at all.
Cat,
[95] Hell-cat, Hitler cat, human,
all-too-human cat,
cat corrupt, infected,
instinct with original sin,
cat of a fallen and perverse creation,
[100] hypocrite with the innocent and limpid eyes –
is nothing desirable
till somebody else desires it?
is anything and everything attractive
so long as it is got by stealing?
[105] Furtive and squalid cat,
green glance, squinted over a cringing shoulder,
streaking hurriedly out of the back door

>   in expectation of judgment,
>   your manners and morals are perfectly abhorrent to me,
> [110]   you dirty little thief and liar.
>   Nevertheless,
>   although you have made a fool of me,
>   yet, bearing in mind your pretty, wheedling ways,
>   (not to mention the four mice and the immature stoat),
> [115]   and having put on my hat to go to the butcher's,
>   I may as well go.

This poem – the first of Sayers's "cat poems" – was published in *Time and Tide*, Volume 24, No. 49 (4 December 1943), p. 994. The poem was also published in an anthology compiled by Mona Gooden and entitled *The Poet's Cat* (London: George G. Harrap & Co., 1947), pp. 95-98. (It is noteworthy that several well-known poets had something to say about cats; it is to be noted, also, that the only *statue* of a celebrity in England to be accompanied by a cat is that of Sayers by John Doubleday erected in Witham, Essex, in 1994). The drawings of "Blitz" by Norah Lambourne are reduced from her original sketches.

The poem was read in a B.B.C. broadcast "Mosaic," on Home Service on 28 August 1949, and again on B.B.C. Overseas broadcast on 10 November 1949.

44.
TARGET AREA (1944)

> *OUR bombers*
> *were out over Germany last night, in very great strength;*
> *their main target was Frankfurt.*
>
>   The grim young men in the blue uniforms,
>   professionally laconic, charting, over the inter-com,
>   the soundings of the channel of death, have carried
>   another basket of eggs to Fräulein Fehmer –
> [5]   I do not know, of course, whether she got them.

Fräulein Fehmer,
thirty-five years ago, when I was at school,
taught the piano
in a little music-room, one of a row of little music-rooms
[10] that lived in the dark passage under the stair
leading to the Lower Fourth;
every music-room
distinguished by the name of a great musician;
every music-room
[15] pouring out a jingle of private harmony
in a jangling discord with the private harmonies of its neighbours.
Fräulein Fehmer was stiffly built,
with a strong square face, lionish, slightly blunted,
as though the hand of the potter had given a gentle
[20] push to the damp clay; she wore eye-glasses,
and a shawl round her shoulders in cold weather; her hair
was straight and dark, combed back over a pad;
she had strong square hands, grasping the keys easily
from middle C to the major third over the octave,
[25] blunt finger-tips and wide flat knuckles; she used
a rather unorthodox
and very powerful action of the whole forearm,
so that the wires sang under her touch like bells.
When she started you on a new piece, she always inscribed
[30] the date neatly above it; when you made mistakes,
stumbling feverishly among the accidentals,
she would say, "Na, na!" in a strong, tart, rebuking
voice. She must be getting an old woman now,
if the grim young men in the blue uniforms
[35] have not cancelled time for her.
                                Fräulein Fehmer's music-room
was named "Chopin"; after her favourite composer;
once or twice in the school year
we were invited to hear her give a recital
[40] of Chopin, after supper. We did not grudge seating the Hall
for Fräulein Fehmer; we recognized that her playing

was unlike that of the other music-mistresses;
no doubt they played well, but Fräulein Fehmer's playing
was music. There is a particular Nocturne
that I cannot hear to this day without thinking of her;
when it is rendered
by celebrated musicians over the ether
I see the red brick walls, the games trophies,
the rush-bottomed chairs, the rows of aspidistras
that garnished the edge of the platform, and Fräulein Fehmer,
gowned in an unbecoming dark-blue silk,
lifting the song from the strings with a squaring of her strong shoulders;
the notes on the wireless are only the imperfect echo
of that performance. Memory and association
count for much, but there is no nostalgic glamour
about my memories; I was timid of Fräulein Fehmer,
and I was not happy at school; – I am sure I am right in thinking
that as a pianist she was exceptional.

        Some years before the war –
this war, I mean – I suddenly had a letter
from Fräulein Fehmer, dated from Frankfurt-am-Main.
In the same pointed script that used to adorn my music-books
she said she remembered England with much affection;
she had heard that I was a writer; she would like to read
something that I had written – would I send her a copy
for old sake's sake? it cost more than she could afford
to order a book from England; times were hard,
it was very hard indeed for musicians to live
in Germany nowadays; "of course," she added,
"I am an ardent Nazi."
      She used to wear
a shawl, as I have said, when the weather was pinching.
  Memory

tells me it was grey. Hitler rose to power
on the despair of the middle classes. I sent her books,
and she thanked me;
for a long time we exchanged polite greetings at Christmas.

Last night our bombers
were out in very great strength over Germany;
Fräulein Fehmer was in the target area.

There are so many things that one does not know –
what, for example, becomes of ageing women
whose skill is rooted in the wrong memories
when death puts on his harness (he bears arms
a *cross crampony*, sable); it may be
that ardent Nazis are not encouraged to play
Polish music.

                Tell me, Fräulein Fehmer,
were you playing Chopin when the bombs went down over Warsaw,
or did the Nocturne ring out for the last time
on the last night of August?
How much of your pittance, tapped by the tinkling hammers,
arduously, out of long stretches of common time,
went up in reek and smoke behind Paul's Churchyard?
Did your grey shawl perish in Russia, frozen
to the aching bone it wrapped, that fearful winter
when the dead stiffened as they fell, in the ghastly
    road from Moscow?
When the great Lancasters,
roaring out of England, making the sky boil like a cauldron,
stooped at last upon Frankfurt from the blackness
    between the stars,
did the old, heartbreaking melody cry to you
Poland's agony through the crashing anger of England?
Did we strike you, perhaps, quickly,
tossing the soul out through rent ribs or merciful

splitting of the skull? Or did you
find yourself suddenly awake at midnight,
[105] peering from the blankets, fumbling for your glasses, to see,
by flare-light and fire-light,
the unexpected precipice by the bedside,
the piano shattered aslant, with all its music
coiling out of it in a tangle of metallic entrails,
[110] dust, books, ashes, splintered wood, old photographs,
the sordid indecency of bathroom furniture
laid open to the sky? Or are you, I wonder,
still waiting the personal assault, the particular outrage,
expiating the world's sin in a passion of nightly expectation
[115] till the unbearable is reiterated
and the promise fulfilled?
The death sent out
returns; I have filled the bombs, loaded the bomb-racks,
built the planes, equipped
[120] the laconic grim young men in the blue uniforms;
for this you learned to play Chopin and I to write
that we might exchange these messages and these replies.
Neither of us can stop what is happening now,
nor would if we could; the discord of private harmonies
[125] must be resolved in the deafening cataract of calamity;
the first to cry "Halt!" utters a cry of defeat,
and makes a breach in the dam, through which the water
floods over the house-tops.

                       This I write
with the same hand that wrote the books I sent you,
[130] knowing that we are responsible for what we do,
knowing that all men stand convicted of blood
in the High Court, the judge with the accused.
The solidarity of mankind is a solidarity in guilt,
and all our virtues stand in need of forgiveness,
[135] being deadly.

Chopin and the old School Hall
were out last night over Germany, in very great strength,
taking messages to Fräulein Fehmer.

This poem appeared in *Fortnightly*, New Series, Volume 155, No. 927 (March 1944), pp. 181-184. Concurrently, it appeared in *Atlantic Monthly*, March 1944, pp. 48-50.

After the war, Sayers discovered Fräulein Fehmer's address and sent her food parcels, books, and clothes.

Line 11, *Lower Fourth* = class in school, usually numbered from Sixth downward; l. 24, *major third over the octave* = obviously a large reach for a pianist, the note at the third interval over eight diatonic degrees; ll. 82-83, *death...bears arms* = heraldic devices; *a cross crampony* = the *Oxford English Dictionary* indicates that this phrase (the last word coming from the French *cramponé* [fixed with crampons]) is said of a cross having a square hook-like bend at the end of each limb, i.e. the swastika; l. 89, *on the last night of August* = i. e., of 1939, the eve of the invasion of Poland by Germany and the start of World War II; l. 92, *Paul's Churchyard* = literally, the enclosed area belonging to St. Paul's Cathedral in London; figuratively, area in the vicinity of the Cathedral; l. 96, *Lancasters* = British bombers in World War II.

45.
AENEAS AT THE COURT OF DIDO (1945)

THE ARGUMENT

A cat, having suffered many misfortunes in an enemy-occupied sea-coast town, at length escapes to a British naval raider, and, after a prosperous voyage, is brought to a sea-port in England.

Quis te, nate dea, per tanta pericula casus insequitur? quae vis, immanibus applicat oris?. . . . non ignara mali miseris succurrere disco.

He said, the lean, hard-bitten Tom
        That from the gunboat came ashore:
"Far is the land which was my home,
        O Queen – a land made glad of yore

"With meat and milk and odorous fish
    And many a rich, warm kitchen smell;
Grief to recall! But, if you wish,
I'll be as those who weep and tell.

"I know not what fierce wrath could urge
    Heaven, or for what obscure offence,
Five years to vex us with the scourge
    Of famine, fear, and pestilence.

"We sickened; plates grew empty; dry
    Our saucers; in the blessed bins
Of temple-rubbish even a fly
    Could find no food; our shrivelled skins

"Clave to our bones; our wailing wives
    Kittened in vacant coal-holes; dead
Were all the holy hearths; our lives
    Dragged godforsaken; nay, worse dread

"Shook us – the ghastly air was filled
    With tales of feline sacrifice,
Of cats on kitchen-altars killed
    To appease the hungry deities.

"From monstrous shapes in midnights dire
    We saw the fearful levin fall;
The high fanes crumbled, and the fire
    Blackened them; through the ruined wall

"Huge starving hordes of mice and rats
    Rushed in; we fought – lo, now, the scars
On ear and eyebrow! but our cats
    Were grown too few, too weak for wars.

"The household oracles fell mute;
    In vain we wailed; the high gods went
Wrapped up in some divine pursuit,
    Preoccupied, indifferent.

"So, when nought else was left to save
    But my sad life, I made my way
Down to the margin of the wave
[40]   By night; and in a hidden bay

"I found a boat and climbed aboard,
    Praying the sea-gods; and my vow
Was heard; celestially oared
    At length we sped, while in the prow

[45] "Curled like a whiting on a shelf,
    I drowsed; the rhythmic beatings smote
Dreamlike, and ceased; I found myself
    Hoist to the davits with the boat.

"And thus I waited still, prepared
[50]   For either fortune, felt the slide
And rolling of the vessel, heard
    The long seas slap against her side;

"Till in good time one sought me there –
    The sleek-coat, tabby, guardian-priest,
[55] Who welcomed me, and led me where
    His foreign gods were set at feast,

"Most high and great and glorious
    With braids of gold; they shared benign
Their holy meal; they said: 'Poor Puss!'
[60]   In accents alien, yet divine.

"For those it now behoves me arch
    My pious back, and ply my paws
With grateful diligence; time's march
    Brings in its train new cults, new laws.

[65] "It may be that my ship is bound
    For some far Latium, where, in joy
Mingled with awe, I yet may found
    A happier race, a taller Troy."

	To whom the Queen: "Heroic soul,
[70]	We too have borne the shocks of Fate:
	There is less cream now in the bowl
	And less tinned salmon on the plate.

	"We too have seen the vengeful brand
	Strike from the sky; but yet we live
[75]	Favoured of Heaven, and what our land
	Can offer you, we freely give.

	"But oh! what impious crime, what scratch,
	What curst and deicidal bite,
	What shrine by filthy feline watch
[80]	Profaned, do such great plagues requite?"

	And he: "Cat's eyes may not avail
	To pierce the awful pantry-door
	Where Justice in her iron scale
	Weighs out the meed of less and more.

[85]	"Enough that some dark deed of shame
	By cats has set all Heaven at odds;
	For these prodigious woes proclaim
	That there is war among the gods."

This poem was privately printed by Sayers as a Christmas 1945 greeting for her friends. The copy transcribed here was presented to Dorothy H. Rowe and signed "Best wishes, D. L. S." It is now possessed by the Bodleian Library, Oxford University, and is cited by permission.

The Latin passage preceding the poem is the well-known speech of Dido in the first book of the *Aeneid*:

> O goddess-born, what doom is pursuing you through so many / Hazards? What violent fate casts you on this harsh coast?.../ Being acquainted with grief, I am learning to help the unlucky. (I. 615, 616, 630, C. Day Lewis translation)

In line 26, *levin* = (archaic) flash of lightning; line 45, *whiting* = a small food fish usually served curled up with its tail in its mouth, as a cat lies curled; line 48, *Hoist to the davits* = the boat was raised up to the ship; lines 57-58, *Most high and great.../ With braids of gold* = naval officers; line 61, *some far Latium* = allusion to the destiny of Aeneas; line 73, *vengeful brand* = aerial bombardment.

Dante

46.
ST. BERNARD'S HYMN TO THE BLESSED VIRGIN IN THE ROSE OF PARADISE (1949)

O VIRGIN MOTHER, Daughter of thy Son,
    Lowliest and loftiest of created stature
    Fixed goal to which the eternal counsels run,

Thou art that She by whom our human nature
[5]   Was so ennobled that it might become
    The Creator to create Himself His creature.

Thy sides were made a shelter to relume
    The Love whose warmth within the timeless peace
    Quickened the seed of this immortal bloom;

[10] High noon of charity to those in bliss,
    And upon earth, to men in mortal plight,
    A living spring of hope, thy presence is.

> Lady, so great thou art and such thy might
> That who needs grace nor seeks it at thy knee
> [15] Lets fly his prayer, but fails to wing the flight.
>
> Not only does thy succour flow out free
> To him who asks, but many a time the aid
> Fore-runs the prayer, such largesse is in thee.
>
> All ruth, all mercy are in thee displayed,
> [20] And all munificence; in thee is knit
> Together all that's good in all that's made.
>
> *Paradiso,* xxxiii 1-21

Prepared as a Christmas greeting for 1949 and privately printed, this translation by Sayers of Dante's *Paradiso* xxxiii, 1-21 in *terza rima* in English was sent to her friends. The entire canto, the last in the *Commedia,* runs to one hundred forty-five lines. A little over a third of the *Paradiso* was, of course, translated by Barbara Reynolds, whose copy of "St. Bernard's Hymn" (autographed and signed by the author: "Love & best wishes to you all from Dorothy L. Sayers") I have been privileged to transcribe here. In the first publication of the *Paradiso* in the Sayers-Reynolds translation, lines 13-15 of Canto xxxiii appear slightly changed and improved in directness:

> Lady, so great thou art and such thy might
> The seeker after grace who shuns thy knee
> May aim his prayer, but fails to wing the flight.

In the "Commentaries" to the final canto of the *Paradiso,* Dr. Reynolds remarks with characteristic clarity that "The Prayer to the Virgin," one of the last two Images of the *Commedia,* offers the occasion in which

> St. Bernard implores her to intercede for Dante that he may attain, now, to the vision of God and that, in his life henceforth, he may, under her protection, persevere in truth and righteousness, his affections and human impulses guarded from unworthiness. The prayer is also a hymn of praise to the Virgin.... In the *story,* the Virgin, from the very beginning, is the gentle Lady who is so moved to pity on Dante's account

that for her sake "high doom is cancelled" (*Inf.* ll. 94-96). She it is who summons Lucy to her side, exhorting her: "Thy faithful votary needs thee, and I commend him to thy care": and Lucy, in her turn, appeals to Beatrice, who swiftly seeks the aid of Virgil, who, alone, at this stage, can speak to, and be heard by, Dante. Now the story has come full circle. Grace, in its various manifestations, has brought Dante from the depths of Hell up to this height. As St. Bernard prays for the Virgin's supreme intercession, all the saints, and Beatrice among them, fold their hands in the vast fellowship of prayer – prayer for one man's need. (*The Comedy of Dante Alighieri the Florentine*, Cantica III, Paradise <Il Paradiso> [Harmondsworth, Middlesex: Penguin, 1962], p. 347).

47.
TORQUATO TASSO TO THE CATS OF ST. ANNE'S (1952)

    Like as at sea, when hurricanes arise
        To vex the turbid waves with boom and jar,
        By night the helmsman to the pole afar,
    Blazing with fires, uplifts his weary eyes;
[5]   So I, storm-tossed by fortune, turn likewise,
        Beautiful puss, to thy mild orbs, which are
        To me as 'twere a blest and double star
    Set for a north in my tormented skies.
    What's next? a kitten? so, my pole would seem
[10]   Complete with Big and Little Bear. O kitties,
        My study-lamps! O pussy-cats, my sweetings!
        So may the Lord deliver you from beatings,
    So may Heaven plenish you with mice and cream,
        Lend me a light by which to pen my ditties.

An epigraph preceding this poem refers to Tasso's circumstance: *(in which hospital he being confined seven years by reason of a disorder in his wits, wrote many verses praying for his release)*. Barbara Reynolds, who located this Petrarchan sonnet for me, writes:

Dorothy found the original in *The Oxford Book of Italian Verse*, second edition, O. U. P., 1952, p. 227. This was reprinted from *Rime*, edited by A. Solerti (Bologna, 4 vols., 1898-1902). Tasso's dates are 1544-1595. In 1565 he joined the court of Ferrara, where he served under Cardinal Luigi d'Este and Duke Alfonso. His principal work, *Gerusalemme Liberata*, was almost complete when, in 1575, he showed signs of mental instability and in 1579 he was put under restraint in the hospital of Sant' Anna in Ferrara. He was there until 1586. It was during this period that he wrote the sonnet to the two cats of Sant' Anna. (From a letter of 9 November 1993.)

48.
[UNTITLED] (1953)

As years come in and years go out
I totter toward the tomb,
Still caring less and less about
Who goes to bed with whom.

This bit of verse by Sayers was in circulation by word of mouth and attributed to her when John Betjeman wrote to her in 1953 "to ask her for the correct version". She approved the four lines above and added "the following textual criticism: 'The alliteration in the second line lends, I feel, a kind of rickety dignity to the whole, as of one tapping slowly along on two sticks; and the rhyme and enjambement at the end of the 3rd line seem to me to usher in the final pronouncement with a more breathless solemnity'" (Reynolds, p. 363).

Well Betjeman might write to her about the "correct" version! The four lines offered by Janet Hitchman in her biography of Sayers (p. 165) show a variant, accompanied by an unsupportable and undocumented judgment: "Her devouring interest in books continued and she was still reading almost everything that was published *except modern novels*" [my italics]), picked up by the third edition of *The Oxford Dictionary of Quotations* (N.Y.: Oxford University Press, 1980) and presented as one of two citations from Sayers while offering this unheard-of "source" *That's why I never read modern novels* (p. 415). The same tenuous position is taken by *The Oxford Dictionary of Modern Quotations*, ed. Tony Augarde (N.Y.: Oxford University Press, 1991), p. 192.

The original Sayers letter to Betjeman (knighted in 1969, Poet Laureate in 1972) is in the Marion E. Wade Center at Wheaton College, Wheaton, Illinois, and the portion transcribed here is cited by kind permission. The date of the Sayers letter is 2 February 1953.

49.
FOR AN EVENING SERVICE (1953)

This hymn is suitable for the Vigil of the / Enlightenment
                              Tune: St. Clement

THE DAY that Nature gave is ending,
    The hand of Man turns on the light;
We praise thee, Progress, for defending
    Our nerves against the dreadful night.

[5] As o'er each continent and island
    The switches spread synthetic day,
The noise of mirth is never silent,
    Nor dies the strain of toil away.

We thank thee that thy speed incessant
[10]   Provides upon this whirling ball
No time to brood on things unpleasant –
    No time, in fact, to think at all.

Secure amid the soothing riot
    Of crank and sound-track, plane and car,
[15] We shall not be condemned to quiet,
    Nor left alone with what we are.

By lavish and progressive measures
    Our neighbor's wants are all relieved;
We are not called to share his pleasures,
[20]   And in his grief we are not grieved.

Thy wingèd wheels o'erspan the oceans,
>   Machining out the Standard Man.
> Our food, our learning, our emotions
>   Are processed for us in the can.

[25] All bars of colour, caste and nation
>   Must yield to movies and the mike;
> We need not seek communication,
>   For thou dost make us all alike.

So be it! let nor sleep nor slackness
[30] Impede thy Progress, Light sublime;
> Nor ever let us glimpse the blackness
>   That yawns behind the gates of Time.

First published among "The Pantheon Papers" in *Punch*, Volume 226 (2 November 1953), pp. 16-19, this poem was published also in America in *The Christian Century*, Volume 71 (3 November 1954), p. 1329. (Other "Pantheon" papers appeared in *Punch* on 6 January 1954, 13 January 1954, and 20 January 1954.) This version is the 1954 *Christian Century* version, although the only differences from the 1953 *Punch* version are that the *Tune* is italicized, the word *plane* in line 14 is preceded by an apostrophe, and the word *neighbor* in line 18 follows the regular British spelling *neighbour*. According to records at David Higham Associates, the poem also appeared in *St. Martin's Review*, note of payment received made on 1 January 1954.

50.
THE COSMOGRAPHERS (1957)

We try (they said) to keep the text reliable,
>   Purged of old travellers' tales, misinformation,
> Myths, and out-moded types no longer viable;
>   One might expect Nature's coöperation
[5] At least, if none from Oxford – where the hand
>   Habitual writes the *stet* of reverence
> Opposite *Here be Monsters*. But with bland
>   Simplicity, which looks like insolence,

> Still slumber in their academic peace
> [10]   The Dinosaurs on beds of amaranth,
> While out of strange, remote, secretive seas
>   Unlettered men fish up the Coelacanth.

This poem appears in a letter from Sayers to Professor C. S. Lewis written on 3 July 1957. It is in the possession of the Marion E. Wade Collection of the Wheaton College Library, Wheaton, Illinois, and cited by permission.

Lewis had been translated from Oxford to Cambridge in 1954 as Professor of Medieval and Renaissance Studies. His inaugural address was entitled "De Descriptione Temporum." George Sayer writes:

> It was an extraordinary occasion. The hall was...crowded....The lecture was a brilliant performance acknowledged by an ovation rarely given to an academic. Its subject developed from his assertion that the great divide in culture and civilization had taken place between the period of Jane Austen and the present day.... He went on to describe himself as a member of the old order. (*Jack: C. S. Lewis and His Time* [San Francisco: Harper & Row, 1988] p. 218)

He apparently captivated his audience by saying, with pronounced irony, that he was a specimen of Old Western Man and that "There are not going to be many more dinosaurs" (p. 281). Sayer asserted that "For weeks afterwards you heard people describing themselves as 'dinos.'"

Following the text of the poem, Dorothy L. Sayers had written:

> There! wedding-present, slightly belated. For "Oxford" read "Cambridge" if preferred, or any other University which cultivates the Humanities & will scan.

Earlier in the letter she had parodied an old church-song by urging Lewis: "Dare to be a Dinosaur [Daniel], / Dare to stand alone."

To the astonishment of many of his acquaintances, Lewis had in the spring of 1956 married in a civil ceremony Mrs. Joy Davidman Gresham, an American divorcée of Jewish and Communist background, in order to give her British citizenship. (This was done much in the pattern and spirit in which W. H. Auden had "married"

Thomas Mann's daughter Erika.) Lewis considered this "marriage" a mere formality to enable Mrs. Gresham to remain in England since her permit to live and to work there could not otherwise be renewed. Later, on 21 March 1957, Lewis and Mrs. Gresham were married in the Churchill Hospital, Oxford, in a religious ceremony (over the expressed displeasure of the bishop on grounds of church law). Mrs. Lewis had been diagnosed as subject to terminal cancer, although she lived until after the death of Dorothy L. Sayers herself.

A *cosmographer* is one who seeks to map the earth or the universe. Sayers evokes a famous feature of ancient maps when she includes the clause *Here be Monsters*. In l. 6, *stet* is Latin for "let it stand," a word often used in the proof-reading of printing; the entire phrase "the *stet* of reverence" has the meaning of lasting respect. *Amaranth* (l. 10) is an imaginary, unfading flower (deriving from the Greek word meaning "everlasting"). *Coelacanth* (l. 12) indicates a fish thought to be extinct, found only in fossil form, until one species was unexpectedly discovered in African marine waters in 1938.

51.
FOR TIMOTHY, IN THE COINHERENCE (1973)

Tutti tirati sono, e tutti tirano.
Paradiso, xxviii, 129

    Consider, O Lord, Timothy, Thy servants' servant.
        (We give him this title, as Thy servant the Pope,
        Not knowing a better. Him too Thy ministers were observant
    To vest in white and adorn with a silk cope.)

[5]   Thy servant lived with Thy servants in the exchange
        Of affection; he condescended to them from the dignity
        Of an innocent mind; they bent to him with benignity
    From the rarefied Alps of their intellectual range.

    Hierarchy flourished, with no resentment
[10]   For the unsheathed claw or the hand raised in correction,
        Small wild charities took root beneath the Protection,
    Garden-escapes from the Eden of our contentment.

    Daily we came short in the harder human relation,
        Only in this obeying, Lord, Thy commands;
[15]   Weekly we washed his feet, meekly he licked our hands –
    Beseech Thee, overlook not this mutual grace of salvation.

    Canst Thou accept our pitiful good behaving,
        Stooping to share at our hand that best we keep for the beast?
        Sir, receive the alms, though least, and bestowed on the least.
[20]   Save us, and save somehow with us the means of our saving.

    Dante in the Ninth Heaven beheld love's law
        Run up and down on the infinite golden stairway;
        Angels, men, brutes, plants, matter, up that fairway
    All by love's cords are drawn, said he, and draw.

[25]   Thou that before the Fall didst make pre-emption
        Of Adam, restore the privilege of the Garden,
        Where he to the beasts was namer, tamer and warden;
    Buy back his household and all in the world's redemption.

> When the Ark of the new life grounds upon Ararat
[30]   Grant us to carry into the rainbow's light,
>   In a basket of gratitude, the small, milk-white
> Silken identity of Timothy, our cat.

Timothy was a cat belonging to Muriel St. Clare Byrne whom Sayers, as a long-time friend, visited often in her London home. The poem was first published in *The Listener*, 15 March 1973, on page 337, after it was read over B.B.C. Radio by Miss Byrne. It was published in the United States later in the year in Rosamond Sprague's *A Matter of Eternity* (Grand Rapids, Michigan: Eerdmans, 1973, pp. 138-139).

The epigraph from Dante's *Paradiso* is paraphrased in line 24. The last word in the title indicates the influence upon Sayers of the theological thought of Charles Williams, with whom she shared great enthusiasm for Dante: "in love all things, not for their own sake, but as images of the Divine." The rhyme-scheme follows the *In Memoriam* stanza of Tennyson, although the line-lengths vary from alexandrine to poulter's measure.

APPENDIX

Abbreviations Used in the Following List

Atl M	=	*The Atlantic Monthly*
Bodl R	=	Bodleian Library; Sayers autograph materials given to Dorothy H. Rowe [MS. Don. e. 172, fols. 17r to 25v]
Bodl UMM	=	Bodleian Library: *Unique Manuscript Magazine*, ed. G. Dixey [MS. Eng. misc. e. 743, pp. 123-4]
Brabazon	=	James Brabazon, *Dorothy L. Sayers: A Biography* (N.Y.: Scribner's, 1981)
BL	=	British Library
Bus H	=	*Busman's Honeymoon* (London: Gollancz, 1937) [the novel] [the drama]
Chr Cen	=	*The Christian Century*
DLSS	=	Dorothy L. Sayers Society
Ev Week	=	*Everybody's Weekly*
Fort	=	*Fortnightly*
Frit	=	*Fritillary*
Gilbert	=	Colleen Gilbert, *A Bibliography of the Works of Dorothy L. Sayers* (Hamden, Conn.: Archon Books, 1978)
GG	=	*Godolphin Gazette*
Hone	=	Ralph E. Hone, *Dorothy L. Sayers: A Literary Biography* (Kent, Ohio: Kent State University Press, 1979)
L L T	=	*Life and Letters To-day*
List	=	*The Listener*
L Merc	=	*The London Mercury*
New W	=	*The New Witness*
Nine T	=	*The Nine Tailors (London: Gollancz, 1934)*
Oxf Bk It V	=	*Oxford Book of Italian Verse*
Oxf Chr	=	*The Oxford Chronicle*
Oxf J I	=	*Oxford Journal Illustrated*

Oxf Mag	=	*The Oxford Magazine*
Oxf P	=	*Oxford Poetry*
Sat West G	=	*The Saturday Westminster Gazette*
Smith C	=	Rare Book Room of the William Allan Neilson Library of Smith College, Northampton, Massachusetts
T L S	=	*Times Literary Supplement*
Wade	=	The Marion E. Wade Collection of Wheaton College, Wheaton, Illinois

LIST AND LOCATION OF SAYERS'S POETRY

1. "The Parliament and the Castle by the Sea" (1909-1910), Brabazon, p. 19
2. "To Alexandre Dumas" (1908), Smith C
3. "Roundel: To a Lady" (1908), Smith C
4. "The Wedding of Porthos" (1908), Smith C
5. "To an English Actor" (1908), Smith C
6. "Stances à ma Maitresse" (1908), Brabazon, p. 25
7. "Drinking Song" (1908), Wade
8. "The Gargoyle" (1908), Brabazon, p. 20
9. "To Florence Mildred White" (1909/1910), Smith C
10. "To Bianca" (1909), Smith C
11. "Anagram" (1909), Smith C
12. "A Farewell" (1910), Smith C
13. "The Death of the Sun" (1910), *GG*, No. 45, p. 11
14. "To Sir Ernest Shackleton" (1910), *GG*, No. 47, p. 21
15. "Captivo Ignoto" (1910), *GG*, No. 47, p. 25
16. "Panache" (1911), Hone, p. 110
17. "A Song of Life" (1911), Letter to Ivy Shrimpton, 24 Apr.
18. "Ode: from the French of P. Ronsard" (1911), *GG*, No. 49, pp. 17-18
19. "Duke Hilary" (1911), GG, No. 49, p. 18
20. "On the Treatment of Actors" (1911), Brabazon, pp. 40-41
21. "To Molière" (1912), Smith C
22. "Peredur" (1912), Wade
23. "The Horn" (1912), Wade
24. "To H. P. A." (1914), Bodl R; Smith C; Wade
25. "The Lytell Geste of Saint Hugh of Oxford" (1914), Bodl R
26. "Inspiration" (1914), Wade
27. "Preface to a Poem" (1914/1915), Wade

APPENDIX

28. "For the Bach Choir" (1914/1915), Wade
29. "The First Gift I Had for You" (1914/1915), Wade
30. "August" (1914/1915), Wade
31. "The Garden" (1914/1915), Wade
32. "Throw It Away" (1914/1915), Wade
33. "Mirth" (1915), *Frit*, No. 64 (March), p. 5
34. "It's a Long Way to the Never Country" (1915), Bodl R
35. "All Who Once upon This Earth" (1915), Bodl R
36. "To Sleep" (1915), Bodl R
37. "Memory" (1915), Bodl R
38. "Rondeau: When Eve Went Out" (1915), Bodl R
39. "Any Girl to Any Man" (1915), Bodl R
49. "Whence Are You, Master Mariner?" (1915), Bodl R
41. "Leander" (1915), Bodl R; Wade`
42. "Fortune Is Fickle" (1915), Bodl R
43. "An Oxford Kalendar for Somervillians" (1915), Bodl R
44. "Socks" (1915), Bodl R
45. "Term-Thoughts in Vacation" (1915), Smith C
46. "Epilogue" (1915), Smith C
47. "Dedication" (1915), Smith C
48. "To a Leader of Men" (1915), *Oxf Mag*, 5 Feb., p. 174; also in *Unique Manuscript Magazine*, 5 Feb. 1916, pp. 49-50, Bodl UMM
49. "To Members of the Bach Choir on Active Service" (1915), *Oxf Mag*, 18 Feb. 1916, p. 194; Bodl R; Wade
50. "It's Well to Be Methodical" [Song of the Bicycle Secretary] (1915), Bodl R
51. "Ballade" (1916), Bodl R
52. "Icarus" (1916), *Oxf Mag*, 5 May 1916, p. 286
53. "Thomas Angulo's 'Death'" (1916) [written under the pseudonym Rallentando], *Sat West G*, 20 May, p. 9
54. "To–" (1916), Smith C
55. "I Will Build up My House," *OP. I* (Oxford: Blackwell, 1916), p. [5]
56. "There Is No Remedy for This," *OP. I*, p. [6]
57. "Alma Mater," *OP. I*, pp. 9-19; Wade; Smith C
58. "Lay: Mummers, Let Love Go By," *OP. I*, pp. 20-31; first published in *Oxf P 1915*, pp. 50-57
59. "The Last Castle," *OP. I*, pp. 32-46; Bodl R; Smith C; Wade
60. "The Gates of Paradise," *OP. I*, pp. 47-53
61. "The Three Kings," *OP. I*, pp. 54-55
62. "Matter of Brittany," *OP. I*, pp. 56-59; Bodl R; published first in *Frit*, Dec. 1915, p. 42

63. "A Man Greatly Gifted," *OP. I*, p. 60
64. "The Elder Knight," *OP. I*, pp. 61-65; Smith C; Bodl UMM
65. "Hymn in Contemplation of Sudden Death," *OP. I*, pp. 66-67; Bodl R; first published in *Oxf Mag*, Nov. 1915, p. 37
66. "Epitaph for a Young Musician," *OP. I*, p. 68; first published in *Oxf Mag*, 25 Feb. 1916, p. 212
67. "Going-Down Play," *OP. I*, p. 69; Wade
68. "To M. J.," *OP. I*, p. 70; Bodl R
69. "Last Morning in Oxford," *OP. I*, p. 71; Wade
70. "Fair Erembours," *Oxf P 1917*, pp. 52-53
71. "Quem Quaeritis?" (1917/1918?), Wade
72. "They Say That No Man Ever Saw Jesus Smile" (1917/1918?), Wade
73. "Jesus, If against My Will," *Catholic Tales and Christian Songs* (Oxford: Blackwell, 1918), p. [3]
74. "Desdichado," *CT & CS*, pp. 7-8
75. "The Triumph of Christ," *CT & CS*, p. 9; Wade
76. "Christ the Companion," *CT & CS*, pp. 10-11
77. "ΠΑΝΤΑΣ ΕΛΚΥΣΩ ", *CT & CS*, pp. 12-13
78. "The Wizard's Pupil," *CT & CS*, p. 14
79. "The Dead Man," *CT & CS*, pp. 15-16
80. "The Carpenter's Son," *CT & CS*, p. 17
81. "The Drunkard," *CT & CS*, pp. 18-19
82. "Justus Judex," *CT & CS*, pp. 20-23
83. "White Magic," *CT & CS*, pp. 24-25
84. "Lignum Vitae," *CT & CS*, p. 26
85. "Christus Dionysus," *CT & CS*, p. 27
86. "Dead Pan," *CT & CS*, pp. 28-29
87. "Rex Doloris," *CT & CS*, pp. 30-31; first published in *New W*, 26 Apr. 1918, p. 591
88. "Sacrament against Ecclesiasts," *CT & CS*, p. 32
89. "Sion Wall," *CT & CS*, pp. 33-34
90. "Byzantine," *CT & CS*, p. 35
91. "Epiphany Hymn," *CT & CS*, pp. 36-37; first published as a Christmas greeting in 1917 (Gilbert, pp. 19, 131)
92. "Carol," *CT & CS*, p. 38
93. "Fair Shepherd," *CT & CS*, pp. 39-40
94. "A Song of Paradise," *CT & CS*, p. 41
95. "Carol for Oxford," *CT & CS*, p. 42
96. "The Mocking of Christ," *CT & CS*, pp. 43-53
97. "The House of the Soul: Lay," *CT & CS*, pp. 54-63

98. "Pygmalion," *Oxf P 1918*, pp. 46-48
99. "Three Epigrams" (1919), Bodl UMM
100. "Ballad" (1919), Bodl UMM
101. "Great Tom," *Oxf J I*, 15 Jan. 1919, p. 1
102. "The Journeyman," *The New Decameron*, I (Oxford: Blackwell, 1919), pp. 25-28
103. "A Sonnet in the Elizabethan Manner," *Oxf Chr*, 6 June 1919, p. 13
104. "Sleeplessness," *Oxf Chr*, 21 Nov. 1919, p. II
105. "A Song of the Web," *Oxf Chr*, 28 Nov. 1919, p. II
106. "Cares of State," *Oxf Chr*, 5 Dec. 1919, p. II
107. "For Phaon," *Oxf P 1919*, p. 50
108. "Sympathy," *Oxf P 1919*, p. 51
109. "Vials Full of Odours," *Oxf P* 1919, p. 52; *Oxf Chr*, 30 May 1919, p. 13
110 "Veronica" (1929/1921?), *The Quorum*, I (n.d.), p. 22; BL
111. "Prayer to the Holy Ghost against Triviality" (1920/1921?), *The Quorum*, I (n.d.), p. 23; BL
112. "The Master-Thief" (1920), The *New Decameron*, II, 76-81
113. "The Sentimental Shepherdess," *Oxf Chr*, 5 Mar. 1920, p. II
114. "Lord William's Lover," *Oxf Chr*, 39 Apr. 1920, p. II
115. "Obsequies for Music," *Lond M*, III (Jan. 1921), 249-253
116. "The Poem," *Lond M,* IV (Oct. 1921), 577
117. "The Mustard Club" (1926), DLSS Archives
118. "On Guinness" (1935), Brabazon, p. 135
119. *Tristan in Brittany* (London: Ernest Benn, 1929); *Modern Languages* I, 142-147, 180-182
120. Bell Mottoes in *Nine T* (London: Gollancz, 1934), "Lord Peter Is Called into the Hunt"
121. "Here Lies the Body of Samuel Snell," *Nine T,* "The Quick Work
122. "Shadowy, Shadowy, Thin & Pale" (1935), unpublished *Cat o' Mary*, Wade
123. "Here then at home," *Gaudy Night* (London: Gollancz, 1935), Chs. XI, XVIII
124. "Ballad of William Parsons" (1936), *Papers Relating to the Family,* pp. 23-28
125. "Auprès de ma Belle" (1937), *Bus H* [play], Acts II, III
126. "My Lady Gave Me a Tiger" (1937), *Bus H* [novel], Ch. I
127. "Songs for Voyce and Lute" (1937), Wade
128. "As Drizling Water Wears the Stone Away" (1937), Wade
129. "Love Is a Jewell, Love's a Toye" (1937), Wade

130. "The Zodiack" (1937), Wade
131. "Ballade for Browne" (1937), DLSS Archives
132. *The Zeal of Thy House* (London: Gollancz, 1937), *passim*
133. "Venetian Saints" (1937, 1938), DLSS Archives
134. *The Devil to Pay* (London: Gollancz, 1939), *passim*
135. "To the Interpreter" (1939), Preface to *The Devil to Pay*
136. "The Prologue," *He That Should Come* (London: Gollancz, 1939), p. [13]-20
137. "Song of the Legionaries," *He That Should Come* (1939), pp. 48, 51, 52
138. "Song of the Greek Gentleman," *He That Should Come* (1939), pp. 66-67
139. "Song of the Jewish Gentleman," *He That Should Come* (1939), pp. 67-70
140. "Song of Mary," *He That Should Come* (1939), p. 78
141. "For Albert Late King of the Belgians" (1940), *L L T*, July 1940, p. [36]
142. "The English War," *T L S*, 7 Sept. 1940, p. 445
143. "The Burden of Ireland" (1941), in Sir John Colville, *The Fringes of Power: 10 Downing Street Diaries 1939-1955* (N.Y.: W. W. Norton, 1985), pp. 327-328, 429
144. "Lord, I Thank Thee–," *London Calling*, ed. Storm Jameson (N.Y.: Harper & Bros., 1942), pp. 293-298; *Britain*, I (Nov. 1942), 37-41
145. "The Makers," *The Man Born to Be King* (London: Gollancz, 1943), pp. 7-8
146. "All They That to the Sea Go Down," *MBtoBeK* (1943), p. 152
147. "Bring Me Garlands," *MBtoBeK* (1943), p. 284
148. "Soldier, Soldier," *MBtoBeK* (1943), p. 304
149. "Aerial Reconnaissance," *Fort*, New Series, Oct. 1943, pp. 268-270
150. "War Cat," *Time and Tide*, Dec. 1943, p. 994
151. "The Map," *Good Housekeeping*, July 1944, p. 1
152. "Target Area" (1944), *Fort*, New Series, March 1944, pp. 181-184; *Atl M*, March 1944, pp. 48-50
153. "Aeneas at the Court of Dido" (1945), privately printed for Sayers; Bodl R
154. *The Just Vengeance* (London: Gollancz, 1946)
155. Trans., Dante Alighieri, "The Heart of Stone" (1946), Convivio 6, Con. 7, Con. 8, Con. 9, privately printed for Sayers
156. "On Punctuation," Janet Hitchman, *Such a Strange Lady* (N.Y.: Harper & Row, 1947), p. 157

157. "From the Catalects of Pussius Catus [I]" (1948), priv. ptd. for Sayers, Bodl R
158. "A Cat's Christmas Carol" (1948), priv. ptd. for Sayers (personal copy)
159. "From the Catalects of Pussius Catus [II]" (1948?), priv. ptd. for Sayers, Bodl R
160. "There Was an Old Man" (1948?), DLSS Archives
161. Trans., Dante Alighieri, *The Divine Comedy: Hell* Harmondsworth, Middlesex: Penguin, 1949)
162. Trans., Dante Alighieri, "St. Bernard's Hymn to the Blessed Virgin," *The Divine Comedy: Paradise*, xxxiii, 1-21, priv. ptd. for Sayers (Reynolds' copy)
163. "Song of Coel," *The Emperor Constantine* (London: Gollancz, 1951), Act II, Scene 1
164. "Poem of Lactantius," *The Emp. Const.*, II, 1
165. "Crispus Reciting Virgil," *The Emp. Const.*, II, 1
166. "Amoebean Contest," *The Emp. Const.*, II, 2
167. "Songs of Arius Supporters," *The Emp. Const.*, III, 2, 3
168. "Pussydise Lost," *Ev Week*, 7 June 1952, p. 27
169. Trans., Torquato Tasso, "To the Cats of St. Anne's," *Oxf B It V*, 2d ed. (1952), p. 227
170. "As Years Come In," Letter to John Betjeman (1953), Wade
171. "For an Evening Service," *Punch*, 2 Nov. 1953, pp. 16-19; *Chr. Cent.*, 3 Nov. 1954, p. 1329
172. *The Story of Adam and Christ* (London: Hamish Hamilton, 1955)
173. Trans., Dante Alighieri, *The Divine Comedy II: Purgatory* (Harmondsworth, Middlesex: Penguin, 1955)
174. "The Cosmographers," Letter to C. S. Lewis, 3 July 1957, Wade
175. Trans., *The Song of Roland* (Harmondsworth, Middlesex: Penguin, 1957)
176. Trans., with Barbara Reynolds, Dante Alighieri, *The Divine Comedy, III: Paradise* (Harmondsworth, Middlesex: Penguin, 1962)
177. "For Timothy, in the Coinherence," *List*, 15 March 1973, p. 377

Nota bene: I have not included here all the juvenilia, nor the doggerel and parody of the early Wimsey, nor the commonplace verse of the clues for the crossword in "The Fascinating Problem of Uncle Meleager's Will"; nor have I listed the salesman's jingles of Montague Egg or Death Bredon, or the proliferation of frivolous limericks which appear in several of the books of fiction; nor have I listed all of the ephemera from Sayers's letters. See my article "From Poetaster to Poet: One Aspect of the Development of Lord Peter Wimsey," *SEVEN*, Volume 10 (1993), pp. 43-58.

INDEX

♣

Aldington, Richard 106
Allen, Hugh Percy 36-45, 49, 53
Auden, W. H. 122, 155
Augarde, Tony 152
Babington, Margaret 9
Barfield, Owen 106
Bates, H. E. 128
Belloc, H. 83
Benson, S. H. xii, 106
Bentley, Phyllis 128
Betjeman, John 104, 152
Betts, Frank 53
Blackwell, Basil xi, 6, 26, 53, 84, 94, 96
Blunden, Edmund 105, 128
Bottom, Phyllis 128
Brabazon, James vii, 3, 24, 106
Brittain, Vera 6, 44, 96
Britten, Benjamin 18
Byrne, Muriel St Clare, 5, 9, 17, 117-118, 126, 157
Campbell, Roy 105
Carroll, Lewis 2
Chesterton, G. K. 84, 90
Chignell, Robert 18
Childe, Wilfrid Rowland 53
Clarke, Col. Ralph ix
Cleobury, Stephen 71
Cole, G. D. H. 61
Cooper, Lettice 128
Cournos, John 105
Crowell, Thomas 81
Dean, Christopher ix, 49, 98, 131
Delafield, E. M. 128
de la Mare, Walter 128
Deschamps, Eustache 61
de Sola Pinto, Vivian 66, 96
Desportes, Philippe 51
de Vigny, Alfred 35

Dixey, Giles 3, 95
Dobree, Bonamy 128
Duff, Esther Lilian 53
Earp, T. W. 53, 61, 96
Eliot, T. S. 9, 104, 128
Fehmer, Fräulein 13, 140-144
Fleming, John Anthony 2, 17
Forest, Arthur 82
Forster, E. M. 128
Gardner, Brian 122
Gielgud, Val 131
Gilroy, Sir John 106
Godfrey, Catherine 3, 26, 44, 70, 78
Gooden, Mona 140
Graves, Robert 6, 104, 128
Gresham, Joy Davidman 155
Guest, Lady Charlotte 32
Haldane, J. B. S. 6, 96
Hamilton, George Rostrevor 105
Hamilton, Mary Agnes 128
Hancock, Simon 18, 71
Hannay, Margaret vii
Hart, Liddell 128
Higham, David 81, 154
Hitchamn, Janet 152
Hopkins, Antony 18
Hughes, Richard 105
Huxley, Aldous 5, 6, 53, 61, 105
Jaeger, Muriel 49, 70, 83
Jameson, Storm 12, 128
Kaye-Smith, Sheila 128
Knight, G. H. 18
Lambourne, Norah ix
Laski, Harold J. 128
Lee, Laurie xiii, 122
Lewis, C. Day xiii, 105, 122, 128, 148
Lewis, C. S. 1, 17, 154-155
Macauley, Rose 128

Mann, Erika 155
Masefield, John 128
McKerrow, R. B. 118
Molyneux, Mrs. K. I. R. 44, 47, 82
Moult, Thomas 122
Murray, Agnes 61
Napier, Frank 119
O'Brien, Kate 128
Priestley, J. B. 128
Reid-Heymann, Stephen 53
Rendall, Elizabeth 53
Reynolds, Barbara vii, ix, xi-xiii, 3, 8, 15, 25, 49, 61, 70, 84, 106, 107, 118, 120, 149, 150-152,
Ridler, Anne 122
Rowe, Dorothy H. 6, 49, 61, 70, 74, 81, 83, 148
Runcie, Lord Robert 71
Sackville-West, Victoria 105
Sassoon, Siegfried 105
Sayer, George 155
Sayers Society, ix, 45, 71
Scott, Robert A. 110
Scott-Giles, C. W. 16, 118
Shackleton, Sir Ernest 25, 26
Sitwell, Edith 105, 122
Sitwell, Osbert 128

Sitwell, Sacheverell 96
Solerti, A. 151
Spender, Stephen xiii, 122
Sprague, Rosamond 157
Squire, J. C. 104, 105,
Streatfield, Noel 128
Swinnerton, Frank 128
Tennyson, Alfred, Lord 158
Thirkell, Angela 128
Thorpe, Lewis 7
Tolkien, J. R. R. 5, 61
Trevelyan, G. M. 128
Vane, Harriet xii, 8, 108-109
Vines, Sherard 53
Waddell, Helen 128
Wallace, D. A. E. 6, 96
Wavell, Lord A. P. 122
Welch, J. W. 131
West, Rebecca 128
Whelpton, Eric 5, 7, 26
Whistler, Lawrence 122
Williams, A. R. 122
Williams, Charles 9, 15, 158
Williams, Harcourt 10, 119
Wimsey, Roger 117-118
Wimsey, Peter xi, 1, 7, 48, 108-109, 110